T0131551

THE WAY OF THE WORLD

THE WAY
OF THE WORLD

Readings in Chinese Philosophy

TRANSLATED AND EDITED BY

THOMAS CLEARY

SHAMBHALA
Boulder
2009

Shambhala Publications, Inc.
2129 13th Street
Boulder, Colorado 80302
www.shambhala.com

Printed in the United States of America

Shambhala Publications makes every effort to print on acid-free, recycled
paper.

Shambhala Publications is distributed worldwide by Penguin Random
House, Inc., and its subsidiaries.

Library of Congress Cataloging-in-Publication Data
The way of the world: readings in Chinese philosophy / translated and
edited by Thomas Cleary.—1st ed.
p.   cm.
ISBN 978-1-59030-738-0 (pbk.: alk. paper)
1. Philosophy, Taoist.   I. Cleary, Thomas F., 1949–   II. Title:
Readings in Chinese philosophy.
B162.7.W53   2009
181'.114—dc22
2009010616

CONTENTS

INTRODUCTION

Once referred to in terms of a Hundred Schools, the colorful spectrum of Chinese philosophy, however diverse in its attitudes and ideas, is typically centered on concrete problems of human life, from the personal to the political, as an interlinking causal chain or circle. A Chinese philosophy is therefore typically presented as something to be practiced, a guiding principle or path to be followed, and so is referred to as a Way.

Sometimes a Way is named by or for a founding figure, historical or legendary; sometimes a Way is defined in reference to a salient conceptual context or practical method. Expressions such as the Way of Nature, the Way of Humanity, the Way of Heaven, and even the Way of Demons thus emerged over time to describe different stages and schools of Chinese philosophy and practice, these terms appearing within the master works themselves as well as in descriptions by observers and analysts.

A great deal of ancient Chinese historical and philosophical literature was lost long ago through the ravages of warfare and the strategic destruction of books and scholars by the First Emperor of China in the third century B.C.E. Having united the warring Chinese states by military conquest, the First Emperor sought to unite the new empire culturally by erasing history and eliminating competing schools of political philosophy, and reducing government to administration of a mechanical rule of law enforced by a policy of deliberately disproportionate punishment that amounted to a program of state terror.

The regime of the first empire soon cracked and shattered under the weight of its own ambitions and oppressions, to be supplanted by a new dynasty, the Han. Initially implementing more relaxed public policies traditionally associated with so-called Huang-Lao or Taoist philosophy, the ruling house of Han sponsored reconstruction of traditional

Chinese culture, including an attempt to retrieve and organize pre-imperial literature.

This collective concentration appears to have played an important part in the hold on the Chinese empire maintained by the ruling house of Han for more than four centuries, even through calamitous civil wars and a major coup d'état midway through its tenure. So central was this era to the formation of the cultural identity of the Chinese empire that the majority nationality in China today is still referred to by the name of this dynasty, as Han.

The Han reconstruction of ancient literature was faced with massive problems of wastage and confusion caused by human destruction and natural decay. The radical reforms of the First Emperor had created a kind of cultural vacuum, an interruption of tradition that could never be completely bridged and was therefore patched with creativity and imagination. Consequently, there never has been a uniform interpretation of the classics among native scholars, even at the lexical level; many famous books are considered reconstructions, forgeries, or composites; and scholars differed among themselves in their categorizations of philosophers into specific schools of thought.

It was in this milieu that the term *Daojia,* typically anglicized as Taoism or Taoist, was coined by the famous historian Sima Qian (ca. 145–86 B.C.E.) to refer to doctrines he describes in these terms:

> The *Daojia* make people's vital spirit unified, acting appropriately without formality, sufficing all people. As for their practical methods, based on the universal order of yin and yang, taking what is good in Confucianism and Moism, distilling the essences of logic and law, they move with the times, change in response to the concrete, establish customs and carry on business in any way appropriate. The instructions are simple and easy to practice; little is done, but with much effect.

The emphasis on adaptation, expressly including the ability to employ what is useful in other doctrines without emotional bias, enabled Taoism to manifest a multitude of forms over the centuries, and to maintain lines of communication through which other traditions absorbed Taoist teachings. Specific inclusion of Confucianism, Moism, logic, and law, moreover, indicates an understanding of Taoism as essentially pragmatic, innocent of the introverted, irrational, and antisocial attitudes occasionally attributed to it by the uninformed and the immature.

The present volume contains original translations of some of the earliest extant texts containing materials associated with the Daojia, accompanied by compositions of later times and a set of famous apocrypha. These works demonstrate different Taoist approaches to the practical dynamics involved in the relationship between the individual and society.

The first set of materials consists of four Taoist chapters from the mammoth collection *Guanzi,* or *Master Guan,* a very prestigious compendium of practical political philosophy. This work has been classified as Taoist, and also as Legalist. The four chapters presented here are called "Inner Work," "Mental Arts" (I and II) and "Purifying the Mind." Generally speaking, these tracts deal with self-government as at once an analogy and a practical prerequisite for leadership.

The writings are not generally believed to be original works of Guan Yiwu (725–645 B.C.E.), under whose distinguished name the large and varied body of work *Guanzi* has been collected. Some commentary has also been formally internalized, suggesting successive authors, yet these four chapters appear to be among the earliest extant works of Taoist philosophy. A story of Master Guan is given in the later Taoist classic *Master Lie* to convey certain principles of political philosophy, and also to illustrate a fine distinction between subjective and objective judgment, and the respective roles of these perspectives in private and public life:

> Guan Yiwu and Bao Shuya were very close friends. They both lived in Qi. Guan Yiwu attended the duke's son Jiu, while Bao Shuya attended the duke's son Xiaobo.
>
> There was a lot of favoritism in the clan of the Duke of Qi, and his sons by his wife and concubines had equal standing. The citizens feared a civil war. Guan Yiwu and Shao Hu fled to Lu in the service of the duke's son Jiu, while Bao Shuya fled to Ju in the service of the duke's son Xiaobo.
>
> Subsequently Gongsun Wuzhi attempted a coup; Qi had no legitimate ruler, and the two sons of the duke fought to take over. Guan Yiwu battled Xiaobo in Ju, during the course of which he shot an arrow that hit Xiaobo's belt buckle.

After Xiaobo had been established as Duke Huan, he intimidated Lu into killing his brother Jiu; Shao Hu committed suicide on that account, and Guan Yiwu was imprisoned.

Bao Shuya said to Duke Huan, "Guan Yiwu is capable; he can govern the state."

Duke Huan said, "He is my enemy; I want to kill him."

Bao Shuya said, "I have heard that an intelligent ruler has no private grudges. If someone can work for his employer, he can certainly work for his ruler. If you want hegemony or kingship, you cannot succeed without Yiwu. You must release him!"

In the end the duke called for Guan Zhong (Yiwu), and the state of Lu returned him to the state of Qi. Bao Shuya greeted him outside the city and removed his fetters. Duke Huan treated him with courtesy and put him in a position higher than the leading Gao and Guo families. Bao Shuya subordinated himself to him. Entrusted with the administration of the state, he was dubbed Father Zhong. Duke Huan subsequently became Overlord.

Guan Zhong once said in praise, "When I was in straits in my youth, Bao Shu and I were once business partners. When it came to dividing the money I gave more to myself, but Bao Shu didn't consider me greedy because he knew I was poor. When I used to plan enterprises for Bao Shu I went bankrupt, but Bao Shu didn't consider me stupid, because he knows that times may be opportune or inopportune. I served in office three times and was discharged all three times by the ruler, yet Bao Shu didn't consider me unworthy, because he knew my time hadn't come. I went to war three times and fled all three times, yet Bao Shu didn't consider me cowardly, because he knew I had an elderly mother. When the duke's son Jiu was destroyed and Shao Hu committed suicide on his account, I accepted imprisonment and disgrace, but Bao Shu didn't consider me shameless, because he knew that instead of being ashamed over a minor sense of duty I was ashamed of not being distinguished throughout the land. The ones who gave me life were my parents, but the one who knows me is Bao Shu."

With this it is customary to cite Guan and Bao as examples of skill in association, and Xiaobo as an example of skill in employing the capable. But there was really no skill in association, really no skill in employing the capable; yet it is not that there is greater skill in association, not that there is greater skill in employing the capable. Shao Hu did not commit suicide by virtue of his capability; he had no choice but to die. Bao Shu did not recommend a savant by virtue of his own competence; he had no choice but to recommend a savant. Xiaobo did not employ an enemy because he was skillful; he had no choice but to employ an enemy.

When Guan Zhong became ill, Xiaobo inquired of him, "Your illness is serious, Father Zhong, and may be fatal. If you become critically ill, who should I entrust with the state?"

Guan Zhong said, "Who do you want?"

Xiaobo said, "Bao Shuya will do."

"No, he won't. He is so puritanical that he won't associate with anyone unlike himself, and once he's heard of a fault in a person he never forgets it all his life. If you let him administer the state, he'll be investigating the ruler above and imposing on the people below. It wouldn't be long before he'd be punished by the ruler."

Xiaobo said, "Then who will do?"

"If there's no alternative, then Xi Peng will do. He is the sort of man whom superiors forget about and inferiors do not disobey. He is ashamed of not being comparable to the Yellow Emperor, and feels compassion for those who are not comparable to him.

"Those who distribute virtue to others are called sages; those who distribute wealth to others are called savants. Those who use sagacity to lord over others have never won people, while those who use sagacity to humble themselves to others have never failed to win people—regarding the state, there is that which they don't hear; and regarding the home, there is that which they don't see. If there is no other choice, then Xi Peng will do."

But Guan Yiwu was not slighting Bao Shu—he could not but slight him. He was not favoring Xi Peng—he could not but favor him. When you favor someone at first, you may wind up slighting them; when you slight someone at first, you may wind up favoring them. The going and coming of favoring and slighting do not derive from oneself.

The next pair of essays translated here was written by another famous political philosopher, Han Fei (ca. 280–233 B.C.E.). These essays interpret portions of the book by Lao-tzu, which was to become a seminal Taoist classic, the *Tao Te Ching*. As a philosopher, Han Fei has been described by scholars as an erstwhile Confucian turned Legalist, but also as interested in Huang-Lao, shorthand for a type of Taoism focusing on doctrines associated with the names of Huang Di, the Yellow Emperor, a key figure of Chinese and Taoist legend, and Lao-tzu, the nominal author of the *Tao Te Ching*. The commentaries of Han Fei translated here, "Interpreting Lao" and "Taking Lessons from Lao," draw on historical anecdotes to illustrate specific applications of maxims of Lao-tzu to the concerns of leadership.

Han Fei lived and died at a critical time in Chinese history, on the eve of the establishment of the first empire. The tragedy of his life and death as told in a twelfth-century preface to his work helps to explain the Taoist element of his philosophy, considering the problems associated with the chronic power struggles that characterized the age:

> Han Fei was an aristocrat of [the state of] Han. He appreciated Legalism, but attributed his roots to Huang-Lao. In person he stammered and could not speak articulately, but he was a good writer. He and Li Si both attended the noble Master Xun, but Li Si considered himself inferior to Han Fei.

Noble Master Xun mentioned here (Xun Kuang/Xunzi ca. 300–230 B.C.E.) is also one of the famous scholar-philosophers of the time. His student Li Si (280–208 B.C.E.), Han Fei's former classmate, became prime minister of the state of Qin, and then of the first empire established by the king of Qin, who became the First Emperor of China. The story continues with a description of the decadence of the state of Han as the reason for Han Fei's writings, and notes the different reactions to his work on the part of the Han and Qin kings, which would prove critical to his fate:

> As Fei saw the state of Han losing territory and weakening, he wrote recommendations to the king of Han, but the latter was unable to apply them. At this point Fei lamented that the government was not recruiting suitable people or putting savants in office, instead promoting fickle and profligate parasites, rewarding them more than they really merited. He thought schol-

ars used literature to confuse law, while knights-errant used weapons to violate prohibitions. Seekers of celebrity were favored in times of ease, while soldiers of fortune were hired in emergencies. Those who were employed were not worthy of support, while those who were supported were not worthy of employment. Those who were honest and not corrupt were not admitted by ministers who were dishonest and devious.

Observing the vicissitudes of gain and loss in the past, he wrote fifty-five essays, [including] "Indignation," "Five Parasites," and "Inner" and "Outer" sets of "Collected Explanations," totaling over a hundred and ten thousand words.

Someone transmitted that book to Qin. The king of Qin, reading "Indignation" and "Five Parasites, said, "Wow! If I could meet this man and associate with him, even if it meant death I wouldn't regret it!"

Li Si said, "This is Han Fei's writing."

When Qin made a blitz attack on Han, Han Fei was not employed at first; then when the situation became serious, Han Fei was sent as an emissary to Qin. The king of Qin liked him, but before he was employed Li Si slandered him to the king of Qin, saying, "Fei is an aristocrat of Han, which now wishes to subordinate all the lords. In the end Fei will be for Han, not for Qin—this is human psychology. Now if you send him back after a long stay without having employed him, you will be bringing trouble on yourself. It would be better to execute him for violating the law." The king of Qin thought he was right, and sent an officer to arrest Han Fei; Li Si sent someone to him with poison so he could kill himself first.

Han Fei wanted to state his case, but he did not get an audience. The king of Qin had regrets afterward and sent someone to release him, but Fei was already dead.

The tragedy of Han Fei highlights the dilemma of political activists and social critics who endangered themselves by exposure to the very corruption they aspired to reform. Intense competition for influence at court, and the extreme sanctions available to rulers against objects of their displeasure, militated against blind belief in the moral imperative, or indeed the practical possibility, of serving society through government office. The image of the conscientious objector, made famous by the classical Taoist author Zhuang Zhou (Chuang-tzu), thus came to play a distinct role in Chinese history.

This particular outlook is dramatized in a Taoist morality play entitled *The Fisherman and the Woodcutter,* written by the great Song dynasty philosopher Shao Yong (1011–1077 C.E.). An expert in the *I Ching,* Shao Yong is credited with a powerful Neotaoist influence on the development of Neoconfucianism. Although recommended for civil service, he refused to accept appointment, in the manner of a Taoist sage. His reasons for refraining from participation in politics may be gleaned from the dialogue in *The Fisherman and the Woodcutter,* wherein he airs his views on human character and the fabric of society.

While some savants like Shao Yong never took up government office as expected of learned men, others went into civil service for a time but then retired from public life, often to do their most creative work. *The Man of Deer Gate: A Letter from Retirement,* written by scholar-recluse Pi Rixiu of the Tang dynasty, exemplifies this type of Confucian-*cum*-Taoist philosophy.

Pi earned the academic degree of Advanced Scholar between 860 and 873 C.E., and held the office of erudite of the Court of Imperial Sacrifices. His sobriquets included Drunken Singing Scholar, Drunken Scholar, and the Wino. While overindulgence in alcohol is traditionally disapproved in Confucianism, highly talented people who succumb to alcoholism, such as the famous poet Li Bo, are typically portrayed in Taoist annals as exiles from heaven who can scarcely endure the atmosphere of earth.

Retiring from office, Pi went into seclusion on Deer Gate Mountain in Hubei, but died during the disastrous rebellion of Huang Chao in the early 880s, which hastened the ultimate end of the long-standing Tang dynasty some twenty-five years later. Pi's letters from retirement were never completed due to his untimely death. In the essay translated here, he reconciles Taoist and Confucian principles, presenting rational explanations of supernatural imagery to emphasize the importance of responsible education.

Whether in or out of public life, Taoist savants were often sought out for counsel by officials at all levels, from local magistrates and provincial governors to major generals and ministers of state, even the emperors and empresses themselves. This advisory role fostered a genre of Taoist literature focused on practical political science, particularly in terms of psychological techniques designed to develop the individual for the requirements, responsibilities, and methods of leadership.

The Taoist sections of *Guanzi* and *Han Fei* may be considered early examples of this genre; a noted neoclassic of this type is the so-called *Silk Text* attributed to the legendary Huang Shi, written by Zhang Shangying (1043–1124 C.E.), a famous scholar, poet, devotee of Chan Buddhism, and high official in the central government of the Song dynasty. The legend of Huang Shi, to whom the famous manual of military strategy known as *Three Strategies*[1] is also attributed, is recounted in the biography of Zhang Liang. Zhang was instrumental in the founding of the monumental Han dynasty in the third century B.C.E., allegedly based on what he learned from Huang Shi. According to the version of this story retold in the Taoist anthology *Alchemists, Mediums, and Magicians*:

> Zhang Liang was styled Zifang. His ancestors were people of the state of Han. When Qin destroyed Han, Liang used his family fortune to hire assassins to kill the King of Qin to avenge Han, as his forbears had been ministers of the state of Han for five generations.
>
> Liang used to study rites in Haiyang. In the east he met the Lord of the Blue Sea,[2] found a strongman, and made an iron mallet weighing one hundred and twenty pounds. When the King of Qin traveled east, Liang and his assassins launched an attack on him, but mistakenly hit an accompanying chariot. The King of Qin was furious, and had the offenders sought in a great hurry.
>
> Liang then changed his name and fled into hiding.
>
> Once Liang was strolling along an earthen bridge when an old man dressed in coarse wool came up to him, dropped one of his shoes off the bridge, then looked at him and said, "Mr. Scholar, go down and get my shoe." Liang was taken aback and wanted to drive him away. But he forced himself to be patient, and went down and got the shoe, presenting it on his knees. The old man took it on his foot and said, "Mr. Scholar, you can be taught.

---

1. Selections from this text can be found translated in *Ways of Warriors, Codes of Kings* by Thomas Cleary (1999).

2. This refers to one of the so-called Isles of the Immortals of Taoist legend.

Meet me here at dawn in five days." Liang thought it strange, but he assented, still on his knees.

Five days later Liang went, but the old man was already there. "Why are you late?" he said angrily.

Five days later, he went at cock's crow, but again the old man was already there. Again he said angrily, "Why are you late?"

Five days later, he went in the middle of the night. After a while the old man also showed up. Pleased, he said, "This is how it should be." Bringing out a book, he said, "If you read this, you'll be a teacher of royalty. After ten years you'll prosper. In thirteen years you'll see me north of Qi; the yellow stone at the foot of Mt. Gucheng will be me." Then he left and disappeared.

When morning came, Liang looked at the book; it was *Taigong's Art of War*.[3] Considering it unusual, he used to study it. He became a soldier of fortune, and used the book to win over Liu Bang.[4] Liu Bang liked it and always applied its tactics, ultimately using them to take over the empire.

The final work translated in this anthology reflects all of the foregoing issues and elements of Taoism in a more complex framework of mental and physical cultivation, combining systems of social and political philosophy with metaphysics and mystical exercises. This is a hybrid text covering a wide range of Taoist thought, a thirteenth-century version of one of the most famous of Taoist apocrypha, *Wenshi's Classic on Reality*. This text is said to have been originally entitled *Keeper of the Pass*, after the author's official post as warden of the pass westward from China to central Asia. The text is traditionally attributed to a figure known as Officer Xi, Keeper of the Pass, an archetypal sage of ancient times who represents an ideal combination of the exoteric and the esoteric, a socially responsible mystic. The reputed author is memorialized in these terms in the Taoist anthology *Alchemists, Mediums, and Magicians:*

> Officer Xi was a grandee of Zhou. Adept at inner studies, he regularly consumed vital essences and practiced secret charity. None of the people of his time knew him.

---

3. Taigong was Jiang Shang, adviser to the founders of the Zhou dynasty.
4. Liu Bang was to found the Han dynasty, which succeeded the Qin.

When Lao-tzu traveled west, Xi perceived his atmosphere in advance, and knew a real human was going to pass through. Looking to stop him, he actually found Lao-tzu. Lao-tzu knew he was exceptional too, and wrote two works for him, on the Way and on Virtue. Afterward he went into the Gobi Desert with him, and ate black sesame seed. No one knows where he ended up.

Lao-tzu is said to have gone west to escape the disturbed conditions in China as the Zhou dynasty progressively lost its cohesion in the middle of the first millennium B.C.E. It is customarily said that Lao-tzu's destination west was India, but the origin of this theme more likely refers to central Asia, which was linked to China by the Jade Route centuries before the Silk Route. The account continues:

Xi also wrote a book, in nine chapters, called *Keeper of the Pass.* Liu Xiang called it murky and inconsistent, vast and very free, yet with models to make people cool and light, not making people crazy. Chuang-tzu also cites his saying, "It is in oneself without abiding, reveals itself in forming things; like water in movement, like a mirror in stillness, like an echo in response, so indistinct it is as if not there, so still it seems clear. Those who assimilate to it harmonize, those who attain it lead; it never precedes people, but always follows people." He is famed as one of the great real people of old. He was originally called Master Wenshi, Beginner of Culture.

The critic Liu Xiang (79–8 B.C.E.) cited here was a distinguished scholar of the Han dynasty, particularly famous in Taoism for his compilation of legends of immortals. His reference to *Keeper of the Pass* implies the existence of this text in some form by Liu's time, but the received version under the title *Wenshi's Classic on Reality* contains a considerable admixture of late Chan Buddhist, Tantric, and Neotaoist material. This feature is typical of a Yuan dynasty work, although the proportions and priorities of elements from different traditions vary widely within the spectrum of Yuan dynasty syntheses and their Song dynasty precursors. The peculiar mix of philosophies and practices presented in this text, plus the prestige of the source to which it is traditionally attributed, have preserved it as an object of special interest in the Taoist canon.

INNER WORK
from Guanzi

The vitality of all beings
is what causes their production.
It produces the five grains below,
and it makes the stars arrayed above.
Circulating between sky and earth,
it is referred to as ghosts and spirits;
stored in the heart it is called the sage.

Therefore people's energy
is as if up in the sky when bright,
as if in an abyss when dark,
as if in the ocean when serene,
as if in the self when agitated.
Therefore this energy cannot be stopped by force,
but can be stabilized by virtue.
It cannot be called by a voice,
but can be welcomed by a tone.
Preserve it respectfully, don't lose it—
this is called developing virtue.
When virtue is developed, wisdom emerges;
all beings are consequently satisfied.

The general rule of mind
is self-replenishment and self-fulfillment,
inherent creativity and inherent productivity.
The causes of failure in this
invariably involve sorrow, delight,
joy, anger, craving, or greed.

If you can detach from sorrow, delight,
joy, anger, craving, and greed,
your mind will then return to clarity.
The inclination of the mind
is to favor peace and tranquillity.
Don't trouble it, don't disturb it,
and harmony will naturally come about.
It is as evident as if by your side,
yet so elusive as to seem ungraspable,
so far reaching as to seem infinite.
This meditation is not remote—
its efficacy is used every day.

The Way is a means of replenishing the body,
yet people cannot be stable;
they go without returning,
come without staying.
No one hears its sound by calculation;
ultimately it is in the mind.
It is obscure, its form invisible,
yet abundantly coming to life together with us.
What does not show its form
or make its voice heard
and yet is orderly in its development
is called the Way.

In general, the Way has no location,
but a good mind rests in love.
When the mind is tranquil
and the mood is orderly,
then the Way can stay.
That Way is not distant—
with it the people produce.
The Way is not alienated—
by it the people know.
Therefore it winds up seeming
susceptible to being given and taken,
yet it is so far reaching
that it seems to end nowhere.

The sense of the Way
dislikes sound and voice;
cultivate the mind to silence sound,
and the Way can be attained.
The Way cannot be expressed verbally,
cannot be seen by the eyes,
cannot be heard by the ears.
That is how to cultivate the mind
and correct the body.
It is by losing this that people die,
by gaining this that they live;
it is by losing this that undertakings fail,
by gaining this that they succeed.

Overall, the Way has no root or stem,
no leaves or flowers.
That whereby myriad beings are born,
and that by which myriad beings are developed,
is called the Way.
The sky controls regularity,
the earth controls stability,
humanity controls peace and quiet.
Spring, autumn, winter, and summer
are the seasons of the sky;
mountains, hills, rivers, and valleys
are features of the earth;
anger and joy are contrivances of humans.

Therefore sages adapt to the times without being altered,
and go along with things without being affected.
Able to be correct, able to be calm,
only then are they able to be stable.
When a stable mind is within,
the ears and eyes are clear,
while the physical frame is sturdy.
Thus it is possible to be an abode of vitality.

Vitality is refined energy;
with energy, the Way comes to life.

With life, there is thought;
with thought, knowledge;
with knowledge, repose.
Generally, the formation of mind is such
that with too much knowledge it loses life.

The ability to exert influence that can unite everyone is
     called genius;
the ability to adapt so as to unify all affairs is called wisdom.
To exert influence without alteration of mood,
to adapt without compromising wisdom,
can only be done by someone capable
of leadership who maintains unity.
If you keep unity without loss,
you can rule all people.
Those who are capable of leadership employ people;
they are not used by people.

The principle of attaining unity
is that when there is an orderly mind within,
then orderly words proceed from the mouth
and orderly behavior is extended to other people;
when this is so, then the whole world is orderly.
When each statement is so fitting
that the whole world accepts,
and each statement is so definitive
that the whole world listens,
this is what is meant by "the public interest."

When you are outwardly incorrect,
your character doesn't develop;
when you are inwardly unquiet,
your mind is disorderly.
Be outwardly correct and embody virtue,
and the benevolence of heaven
and the justice of earth
will spontaneously well forth.

The consummation of spiritual clarity illuminates
     knowledge.

When justice is preserved without deviation in the midst
    of all things,
things are not allowed to confuse official functions,
and official functions are not allowed to confuse
    the mind,
this is called inner attainment.

There is a spirit intrinsic within the body;
going and coming, no one can conceive of it.
Losing it invariably means confusion,
realizing it invariably means order.
Respectfully clean its abode,
and vitality will come of itself.
Think of it with refined ideas,
govern it with calm attention.

With a dignified mien,
be cautious and respectful,
and vitality will reach stability.
When you attain this
and do not abandon it,
your ears and eyes
will not be promiscuous
and your mind will not have other aims.
With the right attitude inside,
everything is in proportion.

The Way fills the world;
wherever there are people,
it is there,
but people cannot recognize it.
Its interpretation in a statement
would see into the heavens above,
plumb the depths of the earth below,
and circulate throughout all regions.

What does interpreting it mean?
It lies in peace of mind.
When one's own mind is orderly,
official duties are then orderly;

when one's own mind is at peace,
then official duties are peaceful.
What brings order to this is mind,
what brings peace to this is mind.
Store mind in mind.
But how can there be another mind
inside the mind?
That mind of mind
speaks before enunciation,
forms after enunciation,
employs after speaking,
governs after employing.
Without governance,
there will be disorder,
and disorder means death.

When vitality is there,
you naturally live,
outwardly comfortable and prosperous,
inwardly treasuring it as a resource;
abundant, peaceful,
it constitutes a fond of energy.
As long as the fond does not dry up,
the physical body will be firm;
as long as the resource is not exhausted,
the senses will be effective.
Then you can plumb heaven and earth
and shelter the whole land,
without confusion inside,
without corruption outside.
When the mind is complete within,
the body is complete outside;
one is not cursed by heaven
or hurt by humans.
This is called a sage.

If people can be upright and calm,
their skin will be relaxed,
their ears and eyes will be clear and bright,

their tendons will be flexible
and their joints will be strong.
Then they can walk the earth carrying the sky,
observe cosmic space and view the great lights.
Being respectful and careful, without deviation,
daily renewing your virtues,
respectfully expressing your way to the four quarters,
is called inner attainment.
That being so,
if you are not regenerated
this is deviation in life.

Generally, the Way requires comprehensiveness and
    thoroughness;
it requires accommodation and relaxation;
it requires firmness and stability.
Keep to the good and don't give it up;
if you pursue excess, the rewards will be slight.
Once you know the extremes,
return to the virtues of the Way.

When a complete mind is within,
it cannot be concealed;
it harmonizes the physical appearance,
and is visible in the complexion.
Greeting people with a good mood
is more endearing than brotherhood;
greeting people with a bad mood
is more harmful than weaponry.
The unspoken voice is swifter than thunder drumming;
mentality and mood are more obvious than sun and moon,
more apparent than father and mother.

Rewards are not sufficient incentive for good,
punishments are not sufficient deterrents to wrong;
the world submits when psychologically won over,
the world obeys when mentally reassured.
Concentrate energy like a spirit,
and all things will be there.

Can you concentrate?
Can you be unified?
Can you discern
what leads to fortune or calamity
without divination?
Can you stop?
Can you be yourself?
Can you refrain from seeking from others,
and find it in yourself?
Think about this,
think about this,
and think about it again.
If you think about it without realization,
ghosts or spirits might communicate it.
This is not the power of ghosts and spirits,
but the consummation of distilled energy.

Thought and inquiry produce knowledge,
laziness and carelessness produce worry,
violence and contempt produce resentment,
sorrow and depression produce sickness.
When sickness is overwhelming,
death ensues.

If you keep longing for something,
you become inwardly suffocated
and outwardly emaciated.
If you don't figure out
what to do about this soon,
your life will leave its abode.

Eating is best not to fullness,
thinking is best not forced;
from that, the balance
of appropriate moderation
will come of itself.

In the production of the human,
heaven produces the vitality,

while earth produces the physicality;
together these make the human.
When they combine, life is produced;
if they don't combine, no life is produced.
When you examine the process of combination,
the vitality is invisible;
its effects are indescribable.

Be balanced and upright,
let your heart be independent.
The issue of order is in the mind;
this is how to prolong life.
If anger is immoderate,
then figure out a way
to do something about it.
Regulate desires,
get rid of the two curses
of exhilaration and rage,
be balanced and upright,
and let your heart be independent.

When people are born
they are invariably balanced and upright;
what causes them to lose this
always involves joy or anger, worry and trouble.
To put a stop to anger, therefore,
nothing compares to poetry;
to get rid of sorrow,
nothing compares to music;
to regulate enjoyment,
nothing compares to decorum;
to maintain decorum,
nothing compares to respect;
to maintain respectfulness,
nothing compares to calm.
When inwardly calm
and outwardly respectful,
you can return to your nature,
and your nature will be very stable.

The general principle of eating
is that excessive fullness is harmful
and physically unhealthy,
while excessive restriction
causes the bones to wither
and the blood to stagnate.
In between fullness and restriction
is called attainment of harmony,
where vitality lodges
and intelligence is born.
When hunger and fullness
are out of proportion,
then figure out a way
to do something about this.
When full, be vigorously active;
when hungry, broaden your thoughts.
When aging, think of the distant future.

If you are not active when you're full,
your body won't be fully energized.
If you don't broaden your thoughts when you're hungry,
you'll keep on hungering relentlessly.
If you don't think of the distant future when you're aging,
you'll quit as soon as you get tired.

Be greathearted and brave,
magnanimous and broad-minded.
Keep physically calm and be unaffected,
and you can keep unified
and cast aside myriad torments.
Don't be seduced by the prospect of gain,
don't be frightened by the prospect of loss.
Be easygoing, relaxed, and humane,
comfortable with yourself as an individual;
this is called a mood like the clouds,
with the will acting like the sky.

Ordinary human life requires some happiness;
with sorrow it loses order,

with anger it loses rectitude.
With sorrow, sadness, delight, and anger,
the Way has no place.
If you like lust, quiet it;
if you encounter confusion, correct it.
Don't pull, don't push,
and fortune will return of itself.
When other ways come on their own,
collaboration is accordingly possible.

Be calm and you'll get it;
if you become excited,
you will lose it.
Spiritual energy is in the mind,
coming and going.
It is so minute there is no inside,
so immense there is no outside.
The reason it is lost
is because of the harm
caused by excitement.
If the mind can keep calm,
its course will spontaneously stabilize.

People who have attained the Way
regulate their intakes and control their output;
there is no corruption in their hearts.
The logic of regulating desire
is that no one gets hurt.

[2]

MENTAL ARTS I
from Guanzi

The existence of mind in the body
is the position of the ruler;
the nine orifices having functions[1]
is the division of offices.
When the mind stays on its proper course,
the nine orifices are in order.
When cravings fill to overflowing,
the eyes do not see forms,
the ears do not hear sounds.
So it is said, "If the superior departs from the proper course,
subordinates fail in their tasks."

Don't run in place of horses,
or you'll exhaust your strength;
don't fly in place of birds,
or you'll wear out your wings.
Don't act before others,
so you can observe their examples.
If you stir, you lose your position;
be calm, and you'll spontaneously succeed.

---

1. The "nine orifices" refer to the eyes, ears, nose, mouth, and unmentionables, generally meaning the physical organs associated with the functions of the senses, breathing, eating and drinking, elimination, and procreation.

The Way is not far, but it is hard to reach the end.
It abides with people, but is hard to get.
Empty out desires, and spirit will enter in;
clean away impurities, and spirit will stay.

Everyone wants knowledge,
but no one seeks the way to knowledge.
Knowledge? Knowledge?
Even if abandoned beyond the seas,
there is no way to alienate it;
but those who seek it cannot abide by it.
Upright people do not seek it,
so they can be empty.

Empty, void, formless—this is called the Way.
Developing myriad beings is called virtue.
Social relations of ruler and subject,
father and son, are called duty.
Elevation and lowering, salutation and deference,
the maintaining of class differences
and the comprehension of relative and stranger,
are called manners.
Singling out people
who are not in accord with the Way,
no matter how slightly,
for execution, confinement, or punishment,
is called law.

It is possible to abide in the Great Way,
but it is not possible to explain it.
But even if people say it is wrong and pay no heed,
if it is not expressed in words
and does not show in the face,
who in the world can perceive its guidance?

The sky is called empty, the earth is called still;
to be thus is invincibility.
Clean your house, then open your doors;

leave the personal and do not speak of it.
Then the light of spirit will thus be present.

When confusion is on the verge of chaos,
calm it down and it will cure itself.
Strength cannot stand everywhere,
intelligence cannot plan for everything.

Things have forms, forms have names.
When naming is done appropriately,
one is called a sage.

So it is imperative to know
the unspoken and uncontrived;
after that one knows the course of the Way.

Different forms vary in configuration;
by not sharing the variant patterns of myriad beings,
it is therefore possible to be a beginning for the world.

The reason people can be killed
is that they dislike death.
The reason they can be disadvantaged
is that they like advantage.
Therefore noble men
are not seduced by likes
or oppressed by dislikes;
they are calm, joyful, uncontrived,
without cunning and motive.
Their responses are not contrived,
their actions are not obsessive.

Error is in subjectivity,
crime is in aberration.
Therefore a ruler who has the Way
appears ignorant in repose,
while his response to others
is like matching them.
This is the way of calm accord.

"The existence of the mind in the body
is the position of the ruler;
the nine orifices having functions
is the division of offices."

The ears and eyes are the organs of seeing and hearing; when the mind takes no part in the operation of seeing and hearing, then the organs effectively keep to their roles. If the mind has desires, things pass by the eyes without being seen, voices reach the ears without being heard. Therefore it is said, "If the superior departs from the proper course, subordinates fail in their tasks." So it is said that "the art of the mind is to control the openings without contrivance; that is why it is called the ruler."

"Don't run in place of horses . . . don't fly in place of birds."

This means not taking away the capacities of the capable, not competing with subordinates.

"Don't act before others."

One who stirs is unsteady, one who rushes is not calm. This means that one cannot observe when acting.

"Position" means where one stands; a ruler of men stands on yin, and yin is calm. Therefore it says, "If you stir, you lose your position." Yin can control yang; if you are calm, then you can control action. Therefore it says, "Be calm, and you'll spontaneously succeed."

The Way is in heaven and earth, so vast there is no outside, so small there is no inside. Therefore it is said, "The Way is not far, but it is hard to reach the end."

Emptiness is not separate from people, but only sages attain the Way of emptiness; so it is said to "abide with people, but is hard to get."

What people of the world are charged with is vitality. When detached from desire, you are clear; when clear, you are calm. When calm, you're vital; with vitality, you're independent. When independent, you're illumined; when illumined, you're spiritual.

Spirit is most important. Therefore if the house is not clean, then a noble person will not stay there. So it is that the spirit will not abide if there is impurity.

"Everyone wants knowledge, but no one seeks it." The means of knowledge is other, but it is known by self. If you do not cultivate it in yourself, how can you know it in an other? If you cultivate it in yourself, no one can falsify; the false hides nothing. Therefore it is said, "Apart from knowledge, how does one seek?" If nothing is hidden, why conjecture? If there is no seeking and no conjecture, there is no thought. If you have no thought, you frustrate falsification.

The Way of heaven is empty in its formlessness. Being empty, it is unrestricted; being formless, it has neither position nor opposition. Having no position or opposition, it pervades all things without changing.

Virtue is the house of the Way; people who attain it are reborn. Knowing how to attain it is accomplished through the vitality derived from the Way. Therefore virtue is attainment; "attainment" means what is attained in order to be so. Since nonfabrication is called the Way, and housing it is called virtue, therefore the Way and virtue are not separate. So speaking of them does not distinguish them; the principle of separation refers to the means of housing.

"Duty" means everyone is where they should be. Courtesy is based on human feelings; connected to the principle of duty, this is what constructs regularity and refinement for it. Therefore "courtesy" refers to having reason. "Reason" means clarifying distinctions to define duties. So courtesy comes from duty, while duty comes from reason, and reason is based on practicality.

Law is the means of equalization, consisting of what cannot but be so. Therefore execution, confinement, and punishment are used to unify. Thus matters are superintended by law. Law comes from political science, political science comes from the Way.

The Way is such that its form is not seen in action, its virtue is not seen in practice. All beings attain thereby, but no one knows the ultimate. Therefore it is said that "it is possible to abide in it but not to explain it."

What no one can say is supreme; what is said without adjustment is response. Response is not something one contrives; that is why it is possible for there to be no adjustment. "Not being circumspect" means going along. Going along is not one's own concern; that is why it is possible to have no circumspection.

"Not being expressed in words or shown in the face" means having no form; "who in the world can perceive its guidance" means it is deep.

The Way of the sky is empty, the Way of the earth is still. Emptiness implies being uninhibited, stillness implies not changing. Not changing implies that there is no error, so it is called invincible.

"Clean your house, then open your doors."

The "house" refers to the mind; the mind is the abode of intelligence, so it is called a house. To clean it means to get rid of the inclination to excess. The "doors" refer to the ears and eyes. The ears and eyes are the means of hearing and seeing.

Things have forms, forms have names; here words cannot exceed actualities, while actualities cannot extend words. Temporarily describing in terms of form, using form to try to name, considering words critically rectifies names. So it is said that "the unspoken speech of sages is response;" "response" means that it is other people who create it. Apprehending the terms and striving for the appropriate response is the way of response.

The way of noncontrivance is accord. Accord adds nothing and subtracts nothing; the art of accord is to make names according to forms. Names are the means by which sages organize myriad things.

People take a stand if they are strong, do their duty if they are good, flourish if they are able, act if they have a motive. Sages have none of this. Being free from it, they are different from other people. Being different, they are empty. Emptiness is the beginning of all things. So it is said, "It is therefore possible to be a beginning for the world."

When people are oppressed by what they dislike, they forget what they like; when people are seduced by what they like, they forget what they dislike. This is not the Way. So it is said, "(Noble men) are not seduced by likes and not oppressed by dislikes." Their dislikes are not irrational, and their likes are not fanatical; so it says, "Noble men are calm, joyful, and not contrived, without cunning or ulterior motive." This means being empty and plain.

"Their responses are not contrived, their actions are not obsessive."

This refers to accord. "Accord" means disregarding yourself and going along with others as a rule. Responding only after being moved to do so is not something contrived; acting for an objective reason is not an obsession.

"Error is in subjectivity, crime is in aberration."

If your subjectivity is involved, you are not empty; if you are not empty, you oppose others. When there is aberration you contrive to survive; when you contrive to survive, you act arbitrarily. Therefore the Way values accord; "accord" means articulating functions according to abilities.

"A noble man appears ignorant in repose" means he is utterly empty; "his response to others is like matching them" means the timing is appropriate. It is like reflections resembling forms, echoes responding to sounds. Thus when people show up he responds, then when they're gone he lets go. "Letting go" means returning to emptiness.

[3]

MENTAL ARTS II
from Guanzi

If you are not formally correct, virtue will not come; if you are not inwardly refined, your mind will be unruly. Be correct in form and cultivate virtue, and everyone will ultimately be won over, coming of their own accord.

No one knows the limit of spirit; it apprehends the whole world, penetrating the four quarters. So it is said, "Don't let the person corrupt the office, don't let the office corrupt the mind." This is called inner virtue.

For this reason, it is only after the mood is stabilized that one returns to sobriety. Mood pervades the person; conduct is the duty to be correct. If what is within one is unattractive, one will not win hearts; if one's conduct is not correct, then the people will not obey. Therefore sages are like the sky, covering nothing privately; they are like the earth, carrying nothing privately. Private interest is what corrupts the world.

When people come with reputations, sages endow them accordingly, and the world is orderly. As long as realities are not violated, they do not create confusion in the world, so the world is orderly.

Concentrate your will, unite your mind; then your perceptions will be accurate, and you'll apprehend evidence of the far distant. Can you concentrate? Can you unify? Can you apprehend what bodes ill or good without divination? Can you stop? Can you withdraw? Can you find it in yourself on your own, without asking others?

So it is said, "Think about it; if you think about it but don't get it, ghosts or spirits will teach it." The power of ghosts and spirits is the consummation of vital energy. Unifying energy so you can transform is called vitality; concentrating on a matter so you can effect change is called intelligence.

Recruitment and selection are means of matching tasks. Changing on reaching impasses is a means of responding to people. If recruitment and selection are not corrupted, change at impasses is not troublesome.

If a noble man who maintains unity maintains unity without fail, he can rule the masses. He illumines like the sun and moon, he organizes like sky and earth. The sage evaluates others, and is not compelled by others. When his mind is at peace, his country is at peace; when his mind is orderly, his country is orderly.

What brings order is the mind; what establishes peace is the mind. When there's an orderly mind within, orderly speech emerges from the mouth, and the tasks of order are provided for the people. Therefore work gets done and the people cooperate, so the common folk are orderly. The reason for discipline is not punishment, the reason for apprehension is not anger. When the people have personal discipline, the common folk are orderly; the basis of the Way is attained.

If attainment does not attain nonbeing, then disorder will ensue even without interference. Whenever those in office profit from being in control, this is not the Way.

The Way of sages seems to be there, yet seems to disappear. If you hold to it and apply it, it will never disappear; if you adapt to the times without being changed, and respond to people without being affected, you can apply it in daily life without alteration.

If people can be correct and calm, their sinews will be strong and their bones sturdy. Those who can carry the great circle can comprehend the great square;[1] those who mirror great clarity see great illumination. Correct and calm without fail, they renew their virtues daily; knowing the world clearly, they penetrate everywhere.

A heart of gold within cannot be concealed; it shows externally in one's appearance, and can be discerned in one's face. If you greet people with a good mood, they are friendly as brothers; if you greet people with a bad mood, this injures worse than weaponry. Unspoken words are more audible than thunder drums.

The manifestation of a heart of gold is clearer than the sun and moon, more attentive and perceptive than parents. In ancient times,

---

1. The circle typically symbolizes adaptation and evolution, while the square symbolizes regularity and order. This imagery alludes to the capacity to change without losing stability, and to maintain stability without losing the capacity to change.

enlightened kings' love of the world was the reason the world could cleave to them; brutal kings' hatred of the world was the reason the world could reject them. Therefore to enrich people is not enough to be considered love, and to punish them is not enough to be considered hate. Enrichment is an outgrowth of love, punishment is an outgrowth of hate.

The life span of people requires rectitude and balance; the reasons for losing these invariably involve joy, pleasure, sorrow, and anger. To control anger, nothing compares to music; to regulate music, nothing compares to courtesy; to preserve courtesy, nothing compares to respect. Those who are outwardly respectful and inwardly calm will surely return to their nature. It's not that there is no profitable business, but they have no thought of profit for themselves; it's not that there is no easy situation, but they have no thought of ease for themselves.

There is a mind within the mind. Ideation precedes speech, formulation follows ideation, thought follows formulation, knowledge follows thought. Generally, the form of mind is such that it loses life with excessive knowledge. Therefore being inwardly collected is considered fundamental; then the spring does not run dry, and outside and inside are effectively connected. As the spring does not run dry, the four limbs are firm; if you can get this to work, you are practicing physical fitness.

So sages, to explain them in one statement, observe the sky above and the earth below.

[4]

PURIFYING THE MIND
from Guanzi

Establish what is appropriate,
Set up what should be;
Make purity fundamental.

Consider time a treasure,
Consider order a norm;
With harmony, it is possible to last.

What is not one's own norm is not done,
even if profitable;
What is not proper for oneself is not practiced,
even if profitable;
What is not one's own path is not taken,
even if profitable.

The best follow Nature,
Those next follow humanity—
if others don't propose,[1]
they do not participate;
if Nature does not initiate,
they do not follow.[2]
Therefore their words are not wasted
and their undertakings do not fail.

---

1. This refers to the immediately preceding "those next" that is next best.
2. This refers to the first mentioned "best." The pattern of reference is the scheme *abba*.

Find out beginnings, calculate realities,
get to the root of their origin.
What is known in the abstract
is sought in the concrete:
focus on their reasons,
and you know their state of mind;
find out how they start,
and you know how to define them.

So when it comes to containing the multiplicity
    of beings,
nothing is greater than heaven and earth;
in terms of influencing beings much,
nothing influences them more than the sun
    and moon.
Of the needs of the people,
none are more urgent than water and fire.
So nature does not derange its seasons
for the sake of one being;
enlightened rulers and sages too
do not bend their rules for the sake of a single
    person.

Nature does what it does,
and all beings experience the benefits;
sages too do what they do,
and the common people experience the benefits.
This is why myriad beings
have equally grown and multiplied.

So it is that the way sages govern
is to calm themselves to deal with it;
when things come up,
definition itself orders them;
accurate definition itself orders them.
If the person is biased, definitions are useless.
When definitions are accurate and laws are complete,
then sages have nothing to do.

Permanent stasis is impossible,
anarchy is impractical;
adapt to changes to decide things,
know the times to formulate measures.

The great are magnanimous,
the petty are narrow;
things have excess and deficiency.

When armies go forth,
they go forth against others;
when those others retaliate,
you've brought it on yourself.

The triumph of arms comes from conciliation;
the emergence of virtue comes from the person.
Therefore it is said that "he who is blessed by spirits
is just toward humans."
Warfare must not be unjust;
those who are strong and arrogant diminish their strength;
those who are weak and arrogant soon pass away.
Those who are strong yet humble and just expand their
    strength;
those who while weak are humble and just escape
    penalties.
Therefore an excess of arrogance humbles,
while an excess of humility exalts.

The Way is such that if one person applies it, excess is
    not heard of,
while if the whole world practices it, lack is not heard of;
this is called the Way.
Take a little of it, and you gain a little fortune;
take a lot of it, and you gain great fortune:
put it into practice completely,
and the whole world will follow.
Take nothing from it, and the people will rebel,
and you won't get away unscathed yourself.

The left is going forth, the right is entering in;
if you go forth without hurting others,
by bringing others in you hurt yourself.[3]

To do things as suitable without auguring day or month,
to carefully discern what bodes well or ill without resorting
    to divination,
is called relaxing physically, earning a reputation while
    remaining at ease.

If you do good things without speaking of good,
things get done, but in retrospect, there's no fame.
The capable have no fame;
they pursue their professions without ado.
Precisely calculating expenditure and income,
observe the people's burdens.
Who can be orderly without law?
Who can initiate without innovation?
Who can finish without finality?
Who can yield without weakness?
So it is said, "Splendid, the rise!"
So it is said, "There is a center, which has a center;
who can attain the heart of the center?"
So it is said, "The successful fall, the famous fail."
So it is said, "Who can relinquish fame and success,
and be the same as everyone else?
Who can relinquish success and fame,
and return to incompleteness?"
While incomplete, value is put on completion;
when complete, value is on incompleteness.
The sun starts setting after high noon;
the moon starts waning once it's full.

---

3. That is to say, an aggressive action will incite retaliation unless it carries enough
force to act as a deterrent. This is not a recommendation but an observation. This is
the reason for the philosophy that states that it is better not even to threaten or imply the use of force, even mental, let alone initiate hostile gestures, because of the
factor of rapid escalation, which may bring on more harm than the original aim of
the aggressive action would have justified even to its proponents.

Followers of fullness lack;
followers of greatness perish.
Who can be selfless themselves?
They compare to the order of heaven and earth.

When people say, "good," don't listen.
When people say, "bad," don't listen.
Hold back and wait;
being empty, don't split;
innocently, be spontaneously pure.

Don't take praise to mean something's done;
examine and question it,
without listening to rhetoric.
When everyone acknowledges it,
good and bad are self-evident.

Something must support the sky,
something must bear the earth:
if nothing supported the sky, it would fall;
if nothing bore the earth, it would collapse:
how much the more so of human beings!
There is something that governs humans,
like the movement of thunder drumming.
What cannot stir itself, something stirs it;
what is that something? What is so:
when you look, you don't see;
when you listen, you don't hear;
it pervades the world, imperceptibly,
not obstructed by it.
Focused in the face,
sensed in the skin,
when they question its comings and goings,
no one knows the time.

It is universal in its rectitude,
resilient in its versatility;
no one can find the origin
of its repeated cycles.

So the mouth produces the voice,
the ears hear, the eyes see,
the hands point, the feet tread;
things have their affinities.

Those who are going to be born are born,
those who are going to die, die;
it may be said there is east and west,
but each dies at home.

Setting up constants, establishing norms,
can you keep your integrity?
Always working on the comprehensive Way,
can you govern others?
This is the reason for recording what is wrong
and speaking of what is neglected.

People of superior sagacity
do not speak nonsense
or give meaningless directions;
when people come to them,
they instruct them, that's all.

What comes out in the speech and voice,
what congeals in the physical appearance,
this is what can be understood;
what does not come out in the voice
or become concrete in physical appearances,
this cannot be understood.
When you can induce arrival,
you can cause survival
and can cause destruction.
So it is said,
"Those who cross it in a boat adapt to the water,
those who are just to others bless their spirits."

There are the fit and the unfit for everything;
if fit, they understand
what cannot be understood by explanation.

Thus when someone skillfully promotes projects,
nobody in the nation knows the interpretation.
Going to do good? Don't keep mentioning it.
Going to do wrong? You'll be condemned to punishment.
Good or not, gaining trust is all there is to it!

Between left and right,
just be exactly centered,
suspended like sun and moon,
without any self.
The alert do not regard the world a worry;
the hasty do not make plans considering all things—
who can give up hastiness to become alert?

It is difficult to articulate the art of law;
it must be promulgated consistently,
without saying too much or too little,
which would facilitate evasion.
So it is said, "What does knowledge know?
What does planning plan?"
What is presented after thorough consideration
others will spontaneously take to.

Self-knowledge is called reflection,
knowing others is called completion.
If knowledge is accurate,
it can help the whole world.
Inwardly solidify it as a unity,
and it is possible to last;
discuss and apply it,
and you can be king of the world.

Once perception of Nature is precise,
you know how to propitiate it,
fertilizing the earth to provide for production.

Can you be like wind and waves,
responding at once to wherever it will go?

So when a son replaces his father,
that is called duty,
but when a minister replaces his sovereign,
that is called usurpation.
How could usurpation be celebrated in song
as was King Wu?[4]
That is why it is said,
"Who can leave eloquence and skill
and return to share the same path
as the multitude of people?"
So it is said, "The more people wish for,
the more their clarity deteriorates;
when the conduct rewarded is cultivated,
the path of kingship is narrow."
Those who put fame and profit to bed
eliminate perils to life.
Those whose knowledge is comprehensive
realize themselves life has obstacles.
It is trying to maintain fullness
that is the danger;
fame filling the world
is not as good as stopping.
As fame progresses the body deteriorates;
this is the Way of Nature.
Don't serve in office
in a state that's fully flourishing,
don't marry your offspring
into a family that's fully flourishing;
don't associate with people
who are arrogant and callous.

The Way is as vast as the sky, as broad as the earth,
weighty as stone, light as a feather.

---

4. One of the founders of the Zhou dynasty, which supplanted the corrupted Shang dynasty. King Wu's father King Wen was a vassal of the Shang. He is celebrated in the classic of song for his humanitarian regime in his own domain of Zhou, winning the allegiance of many other groups, ultimately enabling Zhou to displace the Shang.

What makes people tick
is known to but a few.
So it is said, "How is it that the Way is so close,
yet no one can follow it?"
What a waste of effort it is
to give up the near for the far!
So it is said, "If you want to take care of
    your body,
first know your feelings."
A ruler becomes familiar with the whole world
and judges the body within thereby;
knowing imagery by this,
thus he knows behavior and mentality.
Once he knows behavior and mentality,
then he knows how to nurture life.
Left, right, forward, backward,
all around then back in place:
maintaining dignified standards of conduct,
conforming to ideals,
respectfully greeting those who come—
now those who come will follow his Way,
without deviating or overstepping;
order will then endure.
With harmony, return to the center,
and the body and nature will protect each other.
Unity without exception
is called knowing the Way.
If you want to follow it,
you must make your rectitude consistent
and your discipline stable.

Questioning their goings and comings,
no one knows their timing:
seeking it in Nature,
they posit expectations;
if they aren't mistaken in their expectations,
then they can grasp this.
So it is said, "I speak of the infinity
of Your great light:

the light of the great light
is not reserved,
but people don't take part."

Those who identify
get along with each other,
those who are opposed
obstruct each other.
I observe opposites
who obstruct each other;
that's why I know the similarity
of those who got along in the past.

[5]

INTERPRETING LAO
Han Fei

Virtue is internal, attainment is external. "Higher virtue is not virtuous"[1] means the spirit does not get absorbed in externals. When the spirit does not get absorbed in externals, then the body is whole. Physical wholeness is called virtue in the sense that virtue is mastery of the body.

Generally, virtue is accumulated by not striving, completed by not desiring, stabilized by not thinking, and solidified by not exploiting. If you strive for it and desire it, then virtue has no abode. If virtue has no abode, it is incomplete. If you exploit it and think about it, then it is not solid. If it is not solid, then it is ineffective. When ineffective, you produce virtue; but then virtue has no virtue. Not attaining is thus in possessing virtue. So it is said that "higher virtue is not virtuous; this is how to have virtue." Therefore not striving and not thinking is esteemed as emptiness, in the sense that the mind is not restricted.

Those who lack technique deliberately construe having no striving and no thought as emptiness. Those who deliberately make out having no striving and no thinking to be emptiness always have emptiness on their minds; this is being restricted by striving for emptiness. "Emptiness" means the mind is subject to no restriction; now if you restrict it to contrived striving for emptiness, then it's not empty.[2]

---

1. Passages from *Lao-tzu* are cited by quotations, commonly introduced by a concluding "therefore" or "so it is said." Han Fei's explanations precede or contain the passage he is citing, the focus being on the point rather than the text per se, which was not a sacred scripture in Han Fei's time. His commentary was written before there was a standardized text of *Lao-tzu* in the form of the *Tao Te Ching* divided into segments.

2. Compare the Buddhist Nagarjuna: "Emptiness wrongly conceived destroys the dull." (*Mulamadhyamakarika* 24:11)

The nonstriving of the empty does not take nonstriving to be a constant. Because one does not take nonstriving to be a constant, therefore one is empty. When you are empty, virtue is full; fullness of virtue is called higher virtue. So it is said that "higher virtue has no striving, yet there is nothing it doesn't do."

"Humaneness" means the inner heart joyfully loving humanity. The humaneness of joy at people's fortune and dismay at people's misfortune arises from psychological necessity, not from hopes of reward. So it is said that "higher humaneness acts objectively, without ulterior motive."

"Duty" refers to the tasks of ruler and subject, superior and subordinate; the differentiation of father and son, higher and lower status; interaction with associates and friends; distinctions of relatives and strangers, insiders and outsiders.

For subjects to work for rulers is appropriate; for subordinates to regard superiors is appropriate. For sons to work for fathers is appropriate; for commoners to respect nobles is appropriate. For associates and friends to help each other is appropriate. For relatives to be insiders and strangers outsiders is appropriate. "Duty" refers to what is appropriate; being appropriate, it is done. Hence it is said, "Higher duty is done, and there is purpose to its performance."

Manners are means by which feelings are represented, the cultivated expressions of duties; the interactions of rulers and subjects, of fathers and sons, the means of distinguishing the noble and the lowly, the savant and the slob. There may be consideration in the heart that is not communicated, so hurried steps and humble bows are used to bring it to light; the true heart may be loving, yet unknown, so fine words and elaborated expressions are used to convey it. Manners are means by which external regulation expresses what is within. Therefore it is said that "manners are means by which feelings are represented."

Ordinarily, when people are moved by outside things, they don't know courtesy for their own sake. When common people are courteous, it's because they respect other people; so they are sometimes assiduous and sometimes slack. When noble people are courteous, it is for their own sake, so the spirit of it is considered higher courtesy. Higher courtesy is spiritual, but most people are different, so they cannot respond. Hence, "Higher courtesy is rendered, but no one responds." Even though most people differ, sages still respectfully fulfill all the courtesies of conduct without slacking, so it is said, "they diligently keep them up."

There is accumulation on the Way, and there is achievement in virtue; virtue is the achievement of the Way. There is actualization in achievement, and beauty in actualization; humaneness is the beauty of virtue. Beauty has enrichment, and enrichment has concrete expression; justice is the concrete expression of humaneness. Concrete expression has manners, and manners have artistry; courtesy is the artistry of justice. Hence it is said, "After losing the Way you lose virtue; after losing virtue you lose humaneness; after losing humaneness you lose justice; after losing justice you lose courtesy."

Manners are expressions of sensibilities; artistry embellishes substance. The noble get the sense and leave the expression, preferring substance to embellishment. For those who rely on appearances to express sensibilities are in a bad state of mind; those who need embellishment to discuss substance are substantially degenerate—how can they discuss it?

Fine jade is not colored with pigments, a fine jewel is not decorated with silver and gold; their substance is so fine that nothing can embellish it. Whatever depends on embellishment for currency is not beautiful in substance. Therefore, between father and son, ritual is not yet defined; hence, "ritual is slight."

In general, things do not all flourish at once; yin and yang are examples of this. It is logical that there be mutual give-and-take; punishment and reward are examples of this. When the reality is thick, the appearance is thin; the courtesies between father and son are examples of this.

From this perspective, those whose manners are complicated have less real heart.

So performance of courtesies strives to convey people's plain heart. The way common people perform courtesies, if people respond they readily rejoice, while those who don't respond they censure and resent. Now if the performance of courtesies is to convey people's plain hearts, yet is imbued with some portion of mutual reproach, can there be no contention? When there is contention, then there's confusion. Therefore it is said, "Ritual implies weakening of faithfulness and trust, and seems to be the beginning of confusion."

Going before others, acting before rationalizing, is called precognition, in the sense that precognition has no object and is without mental calculation. How can this be discussed? Zhan He was sitting with a disciple in attendance. An ox bellowed outside. The disciple said, "It's a black ox, but has a white forehead." Zhan He said, "Yes, it's a black ox; the white is on its horns." He sent someone to look at it; as it turned out, it was a black ox with cloth wrapped around its horns.

The art of Zhan He, relative to the mind of ordinary people, was indeed quite cultivated, hence the expression "flower of the Way." When Master Zhan's perception was tested, having an untutored boy look, he too knew it was a black ox with cloth wrapped around its horns. So, to trouble with the perception of a Master Zhan to the same effect as an ignorant boy is called "the beginning of ignorance." Hence it is said, "Precognition is a flower of the Way, and the beginning of ignorance."

A so-called great man means one whose wisdom is great. What is called "abiding by the thick and not the thin" is acting on truth and reality, omitting ritual and appearance. What is called "abiding by substance and not embellishment" means unfailingly focusing on reason, without idle imagination. What is called "leaving that and taking this" means leaving appearances and imaginings, taking to focus on reason, and preferring truth and reality. Hence it is said, "Leave this and take that."

When people have trouble, their minds are apprehensive. When their minds are apprehensive, their conduct is correct. When their conduct is correct, their thinking is thorough. When their thinking is thorough, they get the reasons for things. As their conduct is correct, they don't get into trouble. As they don't get into trouble, they live out their natural years. As they get the reasons for things, they surely become successful in what they do. To live out your natural years is to be healthy and long-lived; certain success in your work means wealth and status. Health, long life, and wealth are called fortune. And yet fortune comes from having trouble. Hence it is said, "Trouble is what fortune is based on, whereby success is achieved."

When people are fortunate, wealth and status are attained. When wealth and status are attained, clothing and food are luxurious. When clothing and food are luxurious, arrogance arises. When arrogance arises, conduct gets perverted and action abandons reason. When conduct is perverse, then death is untimely. When action abandons reason, there is no success. Now when there is the personal hardship of untimely death, and socially no reputation for success, this is tremendous trouble. So trouble originates from having good fortune. So it is said, "Fortune is where trouble lurks."

Those who do things reasonably can accomplish anything. Those who can accomplish anything can achieve as much as the power and status of an emperor, or at least can easily obtain the rewards of prime ministers or generals. Those who initiate actions irrationally, even if they have the power and status of emperor or lord and the land is rich, will still lose their populace and their material resources.

Ordinary people readily initiate arbitrary action with little regard for reason, being so ignorant of the depth and magnitude of trouble and fortune, and the breadth and distance of the Way. So, to admonish people it is said, "Who knows the end?"

There is no one who doesn't want wealth, status, health, and long life, yet no one can escape the troubles of poverty, lowliness, mortality, and premature death. When the heart desires wealth, status, health, and long life, but one is presently poor, lowly, mortal, and short-lived, this means one cannot attain what one wants to attain. Whenever you lose the road you want and go the wrong way, that's called being lost. When you're lost, you can't get where you want to go.

Now people cannot get where they want to go, so they are said to be lost. People's inability to get where they want to go has been so from the separation of heaven and earth to the present. Hence it is said, "People have sure been lost for a long time!"

"Rectitude" means inside and outside correspond, actions and speech match. "Integrity" means to be true to the duties of life and death, disinterested in material goods. "Straightforwardness" means invariable fairness and uprightness in principles, being public minded without bias or factionalism. "Brilliance" means official rank and respectability, being well dressed. Now gentlemen who have the Way, though inside and outside are in accord, do not on that account criticize the frustrated and fallen. Though they maintain self-discipline to the death and think little of material wealth, they do not on that account demean quitters or disgrace the covetous. Though they are upright and not partial, they do not on that account get rid of the biased or penalize the selfish. Though they be in positions of power and well dressed, they do not on that account show off to the lowly or cheat the poor.

What is the reason for that? If those who have strayed from the road are willing to listen to the capable and ask the knowledgeable, then they will not get lost. Now the reason why most people fail when they want to achieve something is that they don't know the principles and are unwilling to ask the knowledgeable and listen to the able.

If most people won't ask the knowledgeable or listen to the able, yet sages insist on blaming them for their troubles and failures, they will be resentful. Ordinary people are the majority, while sages are a minority; a minority does not prevail over the majority, as a matter of numbers. Now if one initiates actions that make enemies of the world, this is not the way to health and long life. That is why action is undertaken with pragmatic guidance and regulation. So it is said, "Be correct but not cutting, be honest without besmirching, be straightforward but not unrestrained, be brilliant but not dazzling."

Perceptivity and intelligence are natural; activity and thought are human. Humans take advantage of natural perceptivity to look, rely on natural intelligence to think. Therefore if looking is forced, the eyes are not clear; if listening is strained, the ears are not clear; if thinking is excessive, cognition is confused. If the eyes are not clear, one cannot tell white from black; if the ears are not clear, one cannot differentiate distinct and muddled sounds; if cognition is confused, one cannot determine grounds of gain and loss.

If your eyes cannot tell white from black, you are said to be blind; if your ears cannot differentiate distinct and muddled sounds, you are said to be deaf; if your mind cannot determine grounds of gain and loss, you are said to be deranged. If you're blind, you can't avoid danger in broad daylight; if you're deaf, you can't discern danger from the rumble of thunder; if you're deranged, you can't escape trouble from the laws of human society.

What books call "governing humanity" means regulating activity and rest and economizing expenditure of thought. What is called "serving Nature" means not using up the power of perception, not exhausting the capacities of intelligence. If you use up and exhaust, there is much expenditure of spirit. When there is much expenditure of spirit, then the troubles of blindness, deafness, and derangement occur. So be frugal with these. To be frugal with these means to be sparing with your vital spirit and frugal with your intelligence. Hence it is said, "To govern humanity and serve Nature, nothing compares to frugality."

Most people's use of spirit is overactive. Hyperactivity means much expenditure. Much expenditure is called extravagance. Sages' use of spirit is calm. Calm means minimal expenditure. Minimizing expenditure is called frugality. Reference to frugality as a technique derives from the principle of the Way; if you can be frugal, you are following the Way and obeying its principle. Ordinary people go from trouble to calamity and still don't know when to quit, so they don't follow the principle of the Way. Sages, even before seeing calamity and trouble form, obediently follow the Way, being empty, amounting to immediate acquiescence. Hence it is said, "What is called frugality is the means of immediate acquiescence."

In those who know how to govern humanity, thinking is calm; in those who know how to serve Nature, the senses are empty. As thinking is calm, virtue does not depart; as the senses are empty, harmonious energy enters daily. So it is called "buildup of virtue." Those who can cause past virtues not to leave while new harmonious energy arrives daily are those who immediately acquiesce; so it is said that "immediate acquiescence is called buildup of virtue."

After buildup of virtue, the spirit is calm; after the spirit is calm, harmony predominates; after harmony predominates, plans succeed; after plans succeed, it is possible to lead a multitude. When you can lead a multitude, then it is easy to overcome adversaries in war; when you easily overcome adversaries in war, your philosophy will top the world; when your philosophy tops the world, it is therefore said that "all are overcome." Overwhelming everyone is based on buildup of virtue; so it says, "Build up virtue, and all are overcome."

When you easily overcome opponents in war, you take possession of the whole land; when your philosophy unfailingly tops the world, then the people follow. When you take over the whole land while getting the people to follow, your art is far reaching; so ordinary people cannot see its beginning or end. Since no one can see the beginning, no one knows the end. So it is said, "When all are overcome, no one knows the end."

When you have a country but subsequently lose it, have a body but eventually destroy it, you cannot be said to be capable of keeping your country or able to preserve your body. If you can keep your country, you can surely secure your territory; if you can preserve your body, you can surely live out your natural years. Only then can you be said to be able to keep your country and preserve your body.

Those who can keep their countries and preserve their bodies invariably have also realized the Way. When you realize the Way, your wisdom is deep; when your wisdom is deep, your understanding is far reaching. When your understanding is far reaching, people at large cannot see where it ends. It is just that ability to cause people not to see where your affairs end—not letting the end of your affairs be seen is to preserve your body and keep your country. So it is said, "No one knows your end; when no one knows your end, then you can thereby keep your country."

In the expression "mother of keeping a country," the "mother" is the Way. The Way gives birth to the art of keeping a country. As the art of keeping a country, it is called the mother of keeping a country. Those who deal with the world by means of the Way construct their lives to last and keep their support forever. So it says, "With the mother of keeping a country it is possible to last forever."

Trees have spreading roots and taproots. Roots are the means by which trees stand and live; spreading roots are the means by which trees sustain life. Virtue is the means by which people construct their lives; income is the means by which people sustain life. Virtue is the means by which people construct their lives; income is the means by which people sustain their lives. Now if you build on truth, you can keep your income forever. So it is said, "Make your roots deep." If you comprehend that Way, your life will lengthen day by day. So it is said, "Make the roots firm." When the root is firm, then life lasts long; when the roots are deep, you see eternity. So it is said, "Make the taproot deep, make the roots strong; this is the way to long life and eternal vision."

If craftsmen repeatedly change their occupation, they lose their efficiency; if artisans repeatedly move and don't settle down, they lose their efficiency. If half a day of one man's work is wasted, then in ten days what five men could accomplish is lost. If half of ten thousand men's workday is wasted, then in ten days what fifty thousand men could accomplish is lost. Therefore when there is repeated change of occupation, the more the people, the greater the deficit.

When laws are changed, profit and harm are altered. When profit and harm are altered, then the people's endeavors change. Changing endeavors is called changing occupation. So from a logical point of view, when you work for a multitude, if you repeatedly disturb them you will not get much done; if you pack up a valuable object but keep shaking the box, you will cause a lot of damage. When you cook small fish, if you stir it repeatedly you rob it of its moisture; in governing a large country, if you repeatedly change the laws the people will suffer on that account. Therefore a ruler who has the Way values tranquillity and doesn't change the laws over and over again. So it is said, "Governing a small country is like cooking small fish."

When people get sick, they esteem physicians; when disasters occur, then they fear demons. When sages are in charge, then the people have few desires; when the people have few desires, their physical energy is peaceful, so their activity is orderly and therefore they seldom suffer disaster or injury. Those who do not personally suffer from growths or tumors, jaundice or piles, and do not suffer the disasters of punishment or execution in the outside world are quite indifferent to demons. So it is said, "For those who govern the world with the Way, its demons are not supernatural." The people in an orderly society do no harm to demons and spirits, and neither are they harmed by them. So it is said, "Not that the demons aren't supernatural, but the supernatural doesn't do harm."

As for the curses of demons, making people sick is said to be demons hurting people, while people's exorcising them is said to be people hurting demons. People violating laws is called people hurting the rulers, while rulers punishing and executing people is called rulers hurting people. If the people don't violate the law, the rulers won't administer punishments. When the rulers don't administer punishments, this is called the rulers not hurting the people. So it is said, "Sages don't hurt the people." When rulers and people don't hurt each other, and humans and demons don't hurt each other, "Neither hurt each other."

When the people do not dare to violate the law, then the ruler does not use punishments internally and does not try to make a profit on their production externally. When the ruler does not use punishments internally and does not try to make a profit on their produce externally, then the people flourish. When the people flourish, their stores are full. When the people flourish and their stores are full, it is said that there is virtue.

Generally speaking, a so-called curse means the soul departs and the psyche is disordered. When the psyche is disordered, it has no virtue. If ghosts don't curse people, their souls don't depart; if their souls don't depart, their psyches are not disordered. When the spirit is not disordered, that is called having virtue. When the ruler keeps the stores full and demons don't derange their psyches, then virtue is all in the people. So it is said, "Neither hurt each other, so virtues combine and return to them," meaning that their virtues interactively fulfill above and below, while both return to the people.

A leader with the Way has no grudge or enmity with neighbors or peers outside, while being of benefit to the people inside. One who has no grudge or enmity with neighbors or peers outside is courteous and just in his treatment of lords abroad; one who is of benefit to his people within works on basics in governing human affairs.

When you are courteous and just to lords, then warfare will seldom occur; when you are attentive to basics in governing the people's affairs, then extravagance will cease. Generally, the reason why horses are used too much is that they serve for the military abroad, while providing for extravagance at home. Now, since a ruler with the Way rarely uses the military abroad and prohibits extravagance at home, the government doesn't use horses to fight battles and pursue the defeated, while civilians don't use horses for distant ramblings and illicit trysts; they concentrate solely on the fields, which need manuring and irrigation. So it is said, "When the world has the Way, running horses are returned for manure."

When human rulers do not have the Way, at home they brutalize their people, while abroad they invade and despoil neighboring countries. Because of brutality in the homeland, the people's production is disrupted; because of incursions abroad, war repeatedly breaks out. When the people's production is disrupted, they have little livestock; when war repeatedly breaks out, soldiers get exhausted. When there is little livestock, there are not enough war horses; when the soldiers get exhausted, the army is in danger. When there is a lack of war horses, then work horses are sent out; when the army is in danger, then close retainers serve. Horses serve an important function for the military, while suburbs refer to proximity; now the means of supplying the army are in work horses and close retainers, so it is said, "When the country does not have the Way, war horses are bred in the suburbs."

When people are greedy, their finances go awry. When their finances are in disorder and they are very greedy, dishonesty prevails because of their greed. When dishonesty prevails, the norms of business are disrupted. When the norms of business are disrupted, then troubles and problems occur. From this perspective, troubles and problems come from a dishonest mind.

A dishonest mind is seduced by what is desirable. When presented, desirable things can induce decent people to act treacherously; withdrawn, they bring disaster on good people. When the treacherous arise, they encroach on weak rulers; when disaster strikes, many people are hurt. So the desirable causes encroachment upon weak rulers above and hurts people below. To encroach on weak rulers above and hurt people below is a great crime. So it is said, "No disaster is greater than the desirable." Therefore sages are not attracted to colors and are not addicted to music. Enlightened rulers disregard amusements and avoid excess finery.

Humans have no fur or feathers, so they cannot fend off cold but by clothing. They don't hang from the sky above and are not attached to the earth below; their digestive system is their root, so they can't live without eating. For this reason, they can't avoid having desire for gain. Unless the desire for gain is allayed, it will make the body uneasy. Therefore sages dress adequately to keep off the cold, and eat enough to satisfy hunger, so they are not uneasy. Ordinary people are otherwise; they may become as great as lords, or at least acquire riches, and yet the uneasiness of wanting to get something doesn't go away. Prisoners may get released, and those sentenced to death sometimes survive, but the uneasiness of those who cannot be satisfied is never resolved all their lives. So it is said, "No calamity is greater than being insatiable."

Desire for gain intensifies anxiety, and when you're anxious, illness develops. When illness develops, intelligence diminishes; when intelligence diminishes, you lose measure. When you lose measure, you act arbitrarily; when you act arbitrarily, calamity and injury strike. When calamity and injury strike while illness afflicts you inside, as illness afflicts you inside, pain and trouble make their way to the surface. When pain and trouble make their way to the surface, pain and suffering mix in the bowels and stomach. When pain and suffering mix in the bowels and stomach, the injury to people is distressing. When distressed, you retreat and take yourself to task. Withdrawing and taking yourself to task also comes from desire for gain, so it is said, "No blame is more distressing than desire for gain."

The Way is the whereby of all things, the standard of all order. Order is the pattern of things that come to be; the Way is that whereby all things come to be. So it is said that "the Way is what orders them."

All things have an order that cannot be disregarded, so the function of order is the regulation of things. Everything has its own peculiar order, but the Way comprehends all; when you consider the order of all things, you cannot but change. Because you cannot but change, there is no constant behavior.

As there is no constant behavior, the forces of death and life are involved. Myriad intellects make judgments therein, myriad things come and go therein; the sky is high thereby, the sun and moon get their regularity thereby; the five constants perpetuate their positions thereby; the stars keep their courses correct thereby; the four seasons control their changing weather thereby. The Yellow Emperor ruled the four quarters thereby; Red Pine organized heaven and earth thereby; sages developed culture thereby.

The Way shares the same wisdom with Yao and Shun, the same madness with the Chariot Grabber; the same destruction with Jie and Zhou, the same thriving with Tang and Wu. Do you take it to be near? It travels to the four extremities. Do you take it to be far? It's always by one's side. Do you consider it dark? It shines with light. Do you consider it light? Its substance is dark, obscure, yet its efficacy produces heaven and earth, its synergy emanates thunder and lightening. Everything in the universe depends on it to exist.

In general, what the Way is like is not to be controlling and not to be formal, but to go along with the times flexibly, according to reason.

All beings die through this and live through this; all beings fail through this and succeed through this. The Way is like water; if the drowning gulp too much they die, if the thirsty drink enough they live. It is like sword and spear; fools use them to act out their anger, so disasters occur; sages use them to execute the violent, so good fortune comes about. So you can die by it or live by it, fail by it or succeed by it.

People rarely regard the images of life, but when they find bones, which are images of death, they consider their patterns to imagine their lives. So the means by which people conceptualize are called images. Now, even though the Way cannot be heard or seen, sages grasp their perception to see its form in terms of context. So it speaks of "formless form, image of no thing."

In general terms, order is the distinction of square and round, short and long, coarse and fine, hard and soft. Therefore we can attain the Way only after order is certain. So it is a certain order that there be survival and destruction, death and life, waxing and waning. As things exist and then perish, one moment alive and the next moment dead, growing at first then waning away, they cannot be called eternal. Only that which was born together with the original separation of sky and earth, and which will neither die nor wane when sky and earth dissolve, can be called permanent.

This permanence does not stop change, and has no fixed order. Having no fixed order, it is not in a constant location; this is why it cannot be spoken. Sages, observing its mystic emptiness and utilizing its universal application, imposed on it the label of "The Way" so it could be discussed. Therefore it is said, "The Way may be spoken, but it is not a fixed course."

Humans begin at birth and end at death; birth is called emerging, death is called submerging. Hence it says, we "emerge at birth, submerge at death." The human body has three hundred and sixty joints, four limbs, and nine openings. These are the main components. The four limbs and nine openings add up to thirteen. The action and repose of the thirteen are all properties of life. These properties are called cohorts, so it says, "the cohorts of life are thirteen." Coming to death, too, the thirteen components all shift over to the domain of death; the cohorts of death are also thirteen, so it says, "the cohorts of life are thirteen, the cohorts of death are thirteen."

People keep being born, and whatever has life must be active. When activity is exhausting, it causes loss. When activity does not cease, this means loss does not cease. When loss does not cease, life is exhausted. The exhaustion of life is called death. So the thirteen components are all grounds of death. Hence it says, "Once people have been born, as long as they're alive, they're active; by activity, all go to a ground of death, of which there are thirteen." Therefore sages care for vitality and value being quiet. These thirteen are more serious than the harm rhinos and tigers can do. Rhinos and tigers have territories, and they're active and rest at certain times. If you avoid their territories and watch out for those times, then you can avoid being hurt by rhinos and tigers.

People only know rhinos and tigers have horns and claws; they don't know all things have horns and claws, and they don't avoid being hurt by everything.

How can this be expounded? When the seasonal rain falls and gathers, and the wilds are empty and quiet, if you venture into the mountains or by the rivers in the morning or evening, then the horns or claws of rhinos or tigers will hurt you. If you are disloyal in government service, readily violating prohibitions, then the claws and horns of penal law will hurt you. If you have no self-discipline when you're living in your hometown, and you hate and love immoderately, then the claws and horns of contention will hurt you. If you are addicted to desires without limit, and your activity and rest are not moderated, then the claws and horns of depletion, swelling, and tumors will hurt you. If you like to use your subjective wits and disregard objective reason, then the claws and horns of penalties will hurt you.

Rhinos and tigers have territories, and myriad injuries have sources. Avoid those territories and block those sources, and you avoid the injuries. So it says, "On land they don't encounter rhinos and tigers." In the mountains they don't depend on defenses to save them from harm.

Generally, weapons and armor are means of preparedness against injury. Those who value life have no angry contentious attitude, even if they're in the military; since they have no angry contentious attitude, then they have no use for protection from injury.

This does not refer only to military forces in the field; sages, too, as they sojourn in the world, have no intention of harming people, so surely no one will harm them; since no one will harm them, they don't prepare protection from people. So it says, "In the army they don't equip themselves with armor and weaponry." They avoid all injuries. So it says, "Rhinos have nowhere to gore with their horns, tigers have nowhere to grab with their claws, weapons have nowhere to wound with their blades." Unfailingly avoiding injury without setting up defenses is the principle of heaven and earth. By virtue of attaining the Way of heaven and earth, it is said, "there is no ground of death." To be active yet have no ground of death is called skill at maintaining life.

Those who love their children are kind to their children; those who value life are kind to their bodies; those who esteem achievement are kind to their work.

The way a kind mother treats a helpless child is to strive to bring about happiness and so try to eliminate troubles. Trying to eliminate troubles, her thought is therefore thorough. As her thought is thorough, she apprehends the reasons for things. As she apprehends the reasons for things, she will surely succeed. Being successful, she carries this out without hesitation. Not hesitating is called courage.

The way sages relate to myriad tasks is entirely like a kind mother thinking for a helpless child. So when they see a necessary course of action, they understand and they do the job without hesitation. As not hesitating is called courage, and not hesitating comes from kindness, so it says, "By virtue of kindness one can be courageous."

The Duke of Zhou said, "If the winter ice is not frozen solid, the growing spring and summer flora will not be luxuriant." Heaven and earth cannot always be extravagant, always be expending; how much the less can humans! So everything must have waxing and waning, all events must involve relaxation and tension. A nation invariably has civil and military offices, government invariably involves reward and punishment. Therefore if intelligent men use their resources sparingly, their houses will prosper; if wise men treasure their spirit, they will be full of vitality. If rulers send their soldiers to war carefully, their populations will be large; and when the population is large, the country expands. So to sum this up it says, "By being sparing it is possible to expand."

Whatever has form is amenable to measurement, amenable to distinction. How can this be expounded? If there are forms, then there are short and long; if there are short and long, then there are small and large; if there are small and large, there are square and round; if there are square and round, there are hard and soft; if there are hard and soft, there are light and heavy; if there are light and heavy, there are white and black. Short and long, small and large, square and round, hard and soft, light and heavy, white and black, are called order; when order is determined, things are readily distinguished. Therefore it is after public discussion that statements will stand; strategists know this.

So if you want to make a circle or a square, you follow the compass or carpenter's square; then the accomplishment of all tasks takes shape. All things have a compass and square; advisors take account of compasses and squares, and sages totally follow the compasses and squares of all things. That is why it says they "do not presume to be leaders of the world."

Because of not presuming to be leaders of the world, no task is undone, no accomplishment is unachieved. But if deliberation is to cover the world, how could that be possible except in a major office? Occupying a major office is called being chief in getting things done. Therefore it says, "Not presuming to be leader of the world, one can therefore be chief in getting things done."

Those who are kind to their children do not dare let them go without food or clothing. Those who are kind to their bodies do not dare to deviate from the law. Those who are kind to the square and the round do not dare give up compass and ruler. Therefore if you are in command of an army and you are kind to the soldiers, then in warfare you'll overcome enemies; if you're kind to tools and implements, then your fortress will be secure. Therefore it says, "Be kind in war, and you'll win; use it for defense and you'll be secure."

Now, those who can keep themselves whole and totally follow the order of myriad things will also have celestial life. "Celestial life" means a living heart. So to consummate the Way for the world is life; if you protect them with kindness, things will be complete and all undertakings will be appropriate. So this is called treasure. Thus it says, "I have three treasures, which I keep and value."

What the *Documents* calls the Great Way is the straight way; so-called putting on of appearances is the crooked way. What is referred to as "esteem for shortcuts" means fine appearances. Fine appearances are part of the crooked path.

"When the courts are frequently swept" means there are frequent trials. When there are frequent trials, then the fields are left uncultivated. When the fields are uncultivated, the granaries are empty. When the granaries are empty, the country is poor. When the country is poor but the people's habits are extravagant, as the people's habits are extravagant, the production of clothing and food stops. When the production of food and clothing stops, the people have no choice but to put on clever deceptions. Putting on clever deceptions implies knowing embellishment; knowing embellishment is called dressing up. When there are frequent trials, the granaries are empty, and yet there are means of habitual extravagance, this is injurious to the country, like stabbing it with a sharp sword. So it speaks of "wearing sharp swords." Those who put on appearances of knowledge, whereby they come to injure the country, are invariably privately rich. As they are privately rich, it says, "goods and money they have in surplus." When there are people like this in a country, then ignorant people inevitably find some way to imitate them. Because of imitating them, petty thieves come to be.

Looking at it from this perspective, when big villains act, petty thieves follow; when big villains call out, petty thieves join in.

The pipes are the leaders of the musical instruments; so where the pipes lead, the chimes and strings follow. As the pipes produce the melody, the other instruments all harmonize.

Now, when big villains act, common people start doing it. When common people start doing it, petty thieves are sure to join in. So those who dress up, wear sharp swords, eat and drink to satiety, and have a superabundance of goods and money are called chiefs of thieves.

Regardless of whether they are ignorant or intelligent, nobody has no priorities, but if they are calm and aloof, they are peaceful and secure.

There is no one who doesn't know where calamity and fortune come from, but if they get what they want and wind up indulging in things, then they'll become deranged. The reason it happens this way is that they are drawn by external things and get deranged by indulgence. If they were calm and aloof, they'd have the right priorities, and if they were peaceful and secure, they'd know what makes for trouble or fortune; but now indulgence changes them and external things draw them. So it says they are "taken."

Perfect sages are not like this: once they have established their priorities, even if they see something they like, it cannot draw them. Not being drawn is called not being taken. Having unified their mental state, even if there is something desirable, their spirits are not moved by it. When the spirit is not moved by anything, this is called not being removed [from the normal state]. When people's descendants comprehend this Way and use it to keep their ancestral shrines from extinction, this is called observance in perpetuity.

In the individual, accumulated vitality is virtue; in the home, money is virtue; in the region, state, and empire, the populace is virtue. Now if you cultivate yourself so that external things cannot disturb your spirit, this is why it says, "Cultivate it in the individual, and that virtue is real." "Real" means that caution is steady. If you govern your home such that useless things cannot affect the budget, then there will be a surplus of money. So it says, "Cultivate it in the home, and that virtue is more than enough." If those who govern regions practice this discipline, then homes with a surplus will increase in number. So it says, "Cultivate it in the region, and that virtue grows." If those who govern states practice this discipline, then regions with virtue will increase in number. So it says, "Cultivate it in the state, and that virtue will be abundant." If those who rule empires practice this discipline, then the lives of the people will all benefit. So it says, "Cultivate it everywhere in the world, and that virtue is universal."

The cultivation of the individual can be used as a standard to distinguish noble people from petty people. The government of a locality, government of a state, and rule of an empire can be used to test what is appropriate and observe waxing and waning; then nothing will be overlooked. So it says, "Observe individuals in terms of individuals, observe homes in terms of homes, observe countries in terms of countries, observe the world in terms of the world. How do I know the world is so? By this."

[6]

TAKING LESSONS FROM LAO
Han Fei

When the world has the Way and there are no urgent problems, that is called tranquillity. Rapid relays are not needed, so it is said, "Running horses are sent back to fertilize the fields."

When the world lacks the Way and aggression is unceasing, standoffs go on for years, lice grow in the armor, birds nest in the tents, and still the soldiers don't come back. So it is said, "War horses are born in the countryside."

When tribal people presented rich fox and panther furs to Duke Wen of Jin,[1] Duke Wen accepted the visitors' hides and lamented, "Here I'm doing wrong myself on account of the beauty of the furs." Now then, as for rulers who did wrong on account of reputation, King Yan of Xu[2] is an example. As for examples of wrongdoing on account of cities and territory, there are Yu and Guo.[3] So it is said, "No wrong is greater than approving desire."

When Baron Zhi[4] annexed Fan, in the process, he kept attacking the state of Zhao. The states of Han and Wei opposed him, and his army

---

1. Duke Wen of Jin became overlord of the feudal lords in the seventh century B.C.E., following the famed Duke Huan of Qi, during the Spring and Autumn period of Chinese history, when competition and conflict among the ancient states intensified after the ruling house of Zhou had lost its premier prestige and power.
2. King Yan of the ancient state of Xu reigned in the time of King Mu of the Zhou dynasty (r. 1001–946 B.C.E.). When King Mu heard that King Yan had the allegiance of thirty-six states, he had the state of Chu attack the state of Xu. King Yan of Xu refused to put up a fight on the grounds that war would bring suffering to his people, and as a consequence he was overthrown.
3. The story appears in the text that follows. The ruler of the state of Yu accepted bribes to allow an army through his territory to attack the state of Guo, then was subsequently attacked and overthrown by that same army on its way back.
4. Baron Zhi was one of the six prime ministers of the state of Jin. He is referred to again in short order.

was defeated and he himself was killed. Pursuing soldiers tore him apart and lacquered his skull and made it into a piss pot. So it is said, "No calamity is greater than not knowing when you have enough."

The Lord of Yu wanted the best horses and the finest jades, and didn't listen to Gongzhi Qi,[5] and therefore lost his country and his life. So it is said, "No fault is more miserable than desire for gain."

For a country, survival is normalcy; rule is then possible. For a body, life is normalcy; wealth and nobility are then possible. If they don't harm themselves with desire, a country won't perish and a body won't die. Therefore it is said, "Knowing when you've had enough is sufficiency."

When King Zhuang of Chu[6] had waged a victorious campaign in Heying, on returning he rewarded Sunshu Ao.[7] Sunshu Ao asked for territory in Han, where the soil was sandy and rocky. The feudal law of Chu was that second-generation ministers could acquire territory; Sunshu Ao alone was the exception. He didn't take his territory for the sake of acquisition, infertile as it was, but for that very reason his descendants continued to remember him even after nine generations. So it is said, "What is well constructed is not demolished, what is carefully held is not lost. Their descendants fete them generation after generation." This was the case with Sunshu Ao.

When control is within oneself, that is called gravity; not getting out of place is called tranquillity. Gravity can master levity, tranquillity can master activity. So it is said, "Gravity is the root of levity, tranquillity is the ruler of activity."

So it is said, "A princely man travels all day without leaving his equipment." A country is a ruler's equipment. [King Wuling of Zhao][8]

5. This refers to the story of Yu and Guo mentioned above. Gongzhi Qi was the one who advised the Lord of Yu against accepting bribes of horses and jades to allow an army right of way through his territory.

6. King Zhuang of Chu was an overlord of the Spring and Autumn era who tried to preserve the Zhou dynasty.

7. Sunshu Ao was prime minister for King Zhuang of Chu. He was distinguished for his contribution to the flourishing of the state of Chu and the hegemony of King Zhuang.

8. King Wuling of the state of Zhao abdicated his throne in favor of his son during the Era of the Warring States, when political perils were at their peak, adopting for himself the sobriquet Father of the Ruler.

handed on his country while he was still alive; that's called leaving his equipment. Therefore even though there was heavenly pleasure, he was aloof; to him, there was no Zhao! King Wuling commanded ten thousand chariots, yet he made light of the world for the sake of his body.

Being powerless is called being lightweight; being out of place is called instability. This is why he was imprisoned while alive, and died.[9] So it is said, "With lightness, subjects are lost; with instability, rulers are lost." This describes King Wuling.

Weight or gravity of power is the deep water of a ruler of men. The power of one who rules men is weightier than what is among those who are subjects; once lost, it cannot be regained. Duke Jian[10] lost it to Tian Cheng,[11] the Duke of Jin[12] lost it to his six prime ministers,[13] and their states perished, and they themselves died. Therefore it is said, "Fish should not be taken out of the depths."

Rewards and punishments are the effective tools of a nation. In the hands of rulers, they control subjects; in the hands of subjects, they overcome rulers. When rulers announce rewards, ministers reduce them for the sake of gratitude;[14] when rulers announce penalties, ministers increase them for the sake of threat. When rulers announce rewards, ministers exploit that power; when rulers announce penalties, ministers take advantage of the threat. So it is said, "The effective tools of a nation should not be shown to others."

The king of Yue went to Wu to study; he observed Wu attacking Qi, thus impoverishing Wu. Once the troops of Wu had defeated the men of Qi at Ailing, they spread out over the river plains and reinforced at Yellow Pond; therefore it was possible to contain them at Five Lakes.

---

9. Having abdicated the throne to his son in 298 B.C.E., Wuling was imprisoned during a rebellion in 296 B.C.E. and starved to death in prison.

10. Duke Jian of Qi was known for callousness toward the populace; he was assassinated in 481 B.C.E.

11. Tian Cheng, a minister of Qi, won popular support for being considerate of the populace.

12. In the late sixth century B.C.E., the ruling house of the state of Jin was riven by internal rivalries, and the reins of government were effectively seized by the chief ministers. In 376 B.C.E. Jin was partitioned into Zhao, Han, and Wei.

13. Baron Zhi, mentioned above, was one of these six prime ministers who took over control of Jin from the duke.

14. That is to say, rewards are made hard to get so that people will be more grateful for them.

So it is said, "If you want to herd them, you must let them spread out. When you want to weaken them, you must let them reinforce."

When Duke Xian of Jin was going to attack Yu, he sent presents of jade and horses. When Baron Zhi was going to attack Jiuyou, he sent presents of carriages. So it is said, "If you want to take, you must give."

To initiate operations when there is no form in order to achieve success worldwide is called subtle understanding.

To adopt a position of being small and weak, and value self-humbling, is called the lacking and the weak overcoming the strong.

Whatever has form, the great must start out small; in anything that goes on for long, the multitude must start out as few. So it is said, "The hardest things in the world must be done while easy; the greatest things in the world must be done while small." That is why those who would govern people deal with the small. So it is said, "Plan for the difficult while it is easy. Do the great while it's small." A thousand-fathom levee will leak on account of an ant hole; a hundred-foot house will catch fire from the smoke escaping through a chink in the chimney. Hence the saying, "When Bai Gui walked the levees, he would plug the holes; when an elder guards the fire, he plasters the chinks."[15] That is why Bai Gui had no problems with flooding, and elders have no problems with fires. These are examples of being careful with what's easy in order to avoid difficulty, respecting the small for the far reaching and great.

When [the physician] Bian Qiao[16] saw Duke Huan of Zhai, he stood there for a while. Bian Qiao said, "You have an ailment at the surface of your skin; if it isn't cured, I'm afraid it will deepen." Duke Huan said, "I don't have anything." When Bian Xiao left, Duke Huan said, "For a physician, curing one who's not ill is deemed success."

Ten days later, Bian Qiao appeared again, saw the duke, and said, "Your illness is in your flesh; if it isn't treated, it will go deeper." Duke Huan didn't respond, so Bian Qiao left. Duke Huan was again displeased.

After ten more days Bian Qiao saw the duke again. He said, "Your sickness is in your gut; if it's not treated, it will deepen further."

---

15. Bai Gui is famous for a debate on waterworks with the Confucian philosopher Mencius.

16. Bian Qiao is supposed to have lived around 500 B.C.E. His fame as a physician is legendary, coming to be synonymous with expertise in medicine.

Again Duke Huan did not respond to Bian Qiao; again Duke Huan was displeased.

Ten days later, Bian Qiao took one look at Duke Huan from a distance and ran away. The duke sent someone after him to question him. Bian Qiao said, "When sickness is in the surface of the skin, it can be reached with baths and ointments. In the flesh, it can be reached with acupuncture. In the gut, it can be reached by antacids. But in the bones and marrow, it's in the hands of fate—nothing can be done for it. Now that it's in the bones and marrow, I have no recourse."

Five days later, Duke Huan was in physical pain, so he sent someone to find Bian Qiao. But the physician had already fled to the state of Qin, so Duke Huan ultimately died.

Therefore the way good physicians cure illness is to attack it when it is on the surface of the skin. They all fight it while it's small.

Misfortune and fortune in affairs also have a skin-surface area; that is why it is said, "Sages go about things early."

Long ago when Prince Zhonger of Jin went into exile, he passed through the state of Zheng, but the Lord of Zheng didn't pay his respects. Shu Zhan admonished him, "This is a prince with integrity; if you treat him well, you can build up goodwill." The Lord of Zheng didn't listen. Shu Zhan then admonished him, "If you're not going to treat him well, you'd better kill him so he won't cause you trouble later." Again the Lord of Zheng didn't listen. Then when the prince returned to his homeland in Jin, he mustered an army to attack Zheng, inflicting a major defeat and taking eight cities.

Duke Xian of Jin used jade to bribe his way through Yu to attack Guo. The grandee Gongzhi objected, "This will not do; without lips, the teeth will be cold. For Yu and Guo to rescue each other is not being merciful or generous; if Jin has destroyed Guo today, Yu is sure to perish along with it tomorrow." But the Lord of Yu didn't listen; he accepted the jade and let the Jin troops through his territory. Once the Jin had taken Yu, on the way back they destroyed Guo.

These two ministers both struggled with what was on the surface, yet their lords didn't take their advice. Thus Shu Zhan and Gongzhi Qi were the Bian Qiaos of Yu and Zheng. But the two lords didn't listen, and as a result Zheng was defeated while Yu was destroyed. So it is said, "What is stable is easy to maintain, what has not begun is easy to plan for."

In ancient times, when King Zhou[17] had ivory chopsticks made, Qizi was afraid because he was sure ivory chopsticks wouldn't go with earthenware, so that would require bowls of rhinoceros horn and jade. Ivory chopsticks and jade bowls wouldn't go with plain food, so gourmet dishes would be required. Gourmet dishes wouldn't be consumed while wearing plain clothes in a reed cottage, so brocades and mansions would be required. "I fear for the end," said Qizi,[18] "so I am afraid of the beginning." In five years, King Zhou made a meat garden where he had roasting spits set up, and built a hill of lees overlooking a lake of wine. Eventually, King Zhou perished because of that. Thus Qizi could recognize trouble for the whole land upon seeing ivory chopsticks. So it is said, "Seeing the small is called clarity."

Gou Qian[19] went to do service to study in Wu. He personally took up arms, and washed horses for the king of Wu. That is how he was able to kill Fu Cha[20] at Gusu.

When King Wen was berated at the royal portal, his face didn't change color; but King Wu arrested Zhou at Muye.[21] So it is said, "Keeping weakness is called strength."

While hegemon, the king of Yue didn't think ill of doing service; while king, King Wu didn't think ill of verbal abuse. So it is said, "The reason sages don't ail is that they don't think ill, so they have no ailments."

A rustic of Song found a raw jade and presented it to Zi Han.[22] Zi Han didn't accept it. The rustic said, "This is a treasure. It should be made into a utensil for a gentleman; it shouldn't be used by a man of

17. This refers to the last king of the Shang dynasty, synonymous with decadence and corruption in Confucian historiography.
18. Qizi, a nobleman of the Shang dynasty, went into self-imposed exile in Korea on account of the corruption of the Shang.
19. Gou Qian was a king of Yue, neighboring state of Wu.
20. Fu Cha was a son of He Lu, king of Wu. He had previously inflicted defeat on Gou Qian.
21. King Wen and King Wu, father and son, were founders of the Zhou dynasty that supplanted the Shang in the twelfth century B.C.E. King Zhou, the last king of the Shang dynasty and still the overlord of King Wen, strove to contain the latter's growing prestige, even imprisoning him for a time. King Wen's son and successor King Wu finally overthrew King Zhou and ended the supremacy of Shang.
22. Zi Han was a grandee of the state of Song in the Spring and Autumn period, known for his integrity and sagacity.

no account." Zi Han said, "You consider jade a treasure. I consider not taking your jade a treasure." So the rustic thought jade desirable, but Zi Han did not desire jade. So it is said, "One who wants not to desire doesn't value hard-to-get goods."

Wang Shou traveled around carrying a bundle of books. He met Xu Ping[23] at Zhou Tu. Ping said, "Occupations are contrived for the sake of living in a particular time. Those who know have no permanent occupation. Books consist of words, words are produced by knowledge. The knowledgeable don't store books. Now why are you alone traveling with a bundle of books on your back?" At this, Wang Shou therefore burned his books and danced on the ashes. So the knowing do not teach by talking, and the wise don't store books. These are excesses of the world, and Wang Shou repeated them. This is study without learning. So it is said, "Study without learning leads back to the excesses of the common man."

Things have normal states; it is because of aberration that they are guided. By going along with the way things are, therefore calm is constructive in terms of efficacy, and action follows the Way.

There was a man of Song who crafted an ivory replica of a mulberry leaf for his lord. It took three years to complete. It was so realistic in every detail—contours, branch and stem, fuzz and luster—that if mixed in with real mulberry leaves it couldn't be distinguished. This man subsequently received a salary from the state of Song for his work. When Master Lie heard of this, he said, "If heaven and earth took three years to make a single leaf, there wouldn't be much foliage on anything!"[24] So, to ride on one individual's body instead of taking advantage of the resources of heaven and earth, to imitate one individual's intelligence instead of following the calculations of logic—these are both examples of "one leaf" behavior.

So, when it comes to crops from winter plowing, the minister of agriculture cannot make demands; as for the abundance of grain in a year of bumper harvest, the laborers cannot resent it. If it were a matter of one individual's strength, then even the minister of agriculture isn't adequate; but when going along with nature, even the laborers

23. According to a commentary on the *Huainanzi,* where this story also appears, Xu Ping was a recluse of Zhou dynasty times.
24. Master Lie refers to Liezi (old spelling Lieh-tzu). This story also appears in the Taoist classic *Liezi* attributed to him, where the replica of the leaf is made of jade.

have a surplus. So it is said, "Rely on the nature of myriad beings, and don't pressure or contrive."

Empty openings are the doors and windows of spiritual illumination. The ears and eyes are exhausted by sound and form, the vital spirit is exhausted by external appearances, so inner autonomy is lacking. When there is no inner autonomy, then even if calamity and fortune are like mountains, you have no way to discern them. So it is said, "Not going out the door, you can thereby know the world; not looking out the window, you can thereby know the course of the heavens." This is called spiritual illumination not departing from its reality.

King Xiang of Zhao learned charioteering from Wang Ziqi. After a while, he had a race with him. The king changed horses three times yet still fell behind each time. King Xiang said, "The technique of charioteering you taught me is incomplete." Ziqi replied, "The technique is complete, but you are overexerting it. What is important in charioteering is that the horses be comfortable with the chariot, and that the driver's mind is in tune with the horses. Only then can you move swiftly and travel far. Now, whenever you fall behind you want to catch up with me, and when you get ahead you're afraid I'll catch up with you. Leading the way or competing for distance, one is either ahead or behind. Now if your sense of ahead or behind is relative to me, how can you be attuned to the horses? This is why you fall behind."

Duke Sheng of Bai[25] was contemplating rebellion once when court closed; his cane was upside down, and the sharp tip pierced his chin; blood flowed to the ground, but he still didn't notice. A man of Zheng heard of this and said, "Forgetting his chin? How is that forgetfulness?"[26] So it is said, "The further out one goes, the less one's knowledge." This means that when the intellect comprehends the remote, what it misses is nearby. This is why sages do not always travel; they are capable of knowing everything. So it is said, "They know without going." They can view everything, so it is said, "They understand without seeing." They initiate activities according to the season, accomplish works based on resources available, use the capabilities of all beings to gain benefits beyond; so it is said, "They succeed without trying."

---

25. Duke Sheng of Bai died in 497 B.C.E. He was a grandee of Chu.
26. This story is also cited in *Liezi*. According to the earliest commentary on *Liezi*, there were many savants residing in the state of Zheng, including Master Lie himself.

When King Zhuang of Chu governed, for three years he issued no orders and took no administrative actions. The minister of the right Yang Yuzuo secretly said to the king, "There is a bird perched on a hill to the south; for three years it hasn't spread its wings, flown, or called. It has been silent, as if mute. What is it named?"

The king said, "It hasn't spread its wings, to see to it that the feathers mature. It doesn't fly or call, so it can observe the standards of the people. Though it hasn't flown, when it does it will surely fly to the sky; though it hasn't called, when it does it will surely startle people. You interpret this. I know it." After another half year of inaction, he began to supervise the administration personally, firing ten and hiring nine, executing five great ministers and promoting six men of integrity; then the state became very orderly. He raised an army to punish Qi, defeating them in Xu province, and beat Jin at Heying. Convening the lords in Song, he finally ruled the world.[27]

King Zhuang didn't compromise what was good for the sake of something small, therefore he acquired a great reputation; he didn't reveal directions too early, therefore he had great success. So it is said, "A great vessel takes a long time to complete; a great voice is rarely heard."

When King Zhuang of Chu wanted to attack Yue, Tuzi objected, "Why would Your Majesty attack Yue?" The king said, "The government is in chaos, and the military is weak." Tuzi said, "I may be stupid, but I'm troubled about this. Intelligence is like eyes: we can see things over a hundred paces away, but we can't see our own eyelashes. Your army will itself be defeated by Qin and Jin, losing hundreds of miles of territory; this is weakness in the military. Zhuang Xiqiao is committing robberies in your territory, yet the police can't stop him; this is chaos in government. Your weakness and disorder are not less than those of Yue. If you want to attack Yue, this is an example of intelligence being like eyes." The king then gave up the idea. So the difficulty of knowledge is not in seeing others, but in seeing oneself. So it is said, "Seeing yourself is called enlightenment."

Zixia saw Master Zeng.[28] Master Zeng said, "Why have you gained weight?" Zixia said, "I've gained weight because of victory in battle."

---

27. This means he became the overlord or hegemon of the feudal lords of the disintegrating Zhou dynasty.

28. These two were both distinguished disciples of Confucius.

Master Zeng said, "What do you mean?" Zixia said, "In private life I saw the righteousness of the ancient kings and considered that success; in public life I saw the pleasure of prosperity and nobility, and also considered that success. These two battled inside my chest, and before I knew which would win I lost weight because of it. Now the righteousness of the ancient kings has won, so I've gained weight." So the difficulty in ambition is not in overcoming others, but in overcoming oneself. So it is said, "Overcoming oneself is called strength."

King Wen of Zhou had a jade scepter. King Zhou of Shang sent Jiao Li to ask for it.[29] King Wen wouldn't give it to him. Then Pi Zhong came asking for it, and King Wen gave it to him. That was because Jiao Li was a savant while Pi Zhong was unprincipled; King Wen didn't want savants to realize ambitions, so he gave it to Pi Zhong. When King Wen hired his mentor at a river's edge,[30] it was because he valued him; when he enriched Pi Zhong with the jade scepter, it was because he had spared it. So it is said, "Not valuing one's teacher, not sparing one's material goods, even if knowingly, is very mistaken. This is referred to as an essential subtlety."

29. This is another example of King Zhou of Shang trying to bully and humiliate King Wen of Zhou, as alluded to above, where King Wen's forbearance is represented as instrumental in the ultimate overthrow of King Zhou by King Wen's son King Wu.
30. This refers to the famous Lu Shang. King Wen, at the time entitled Baron of the West under the Shang dynasty, encountered Lu, a savant in rustic retirement, while on a hunting expedition.

[7]

The Fisherman and the Woodcutter

Shao Yong

A fisherman said to a woodcutter, "When the world is on the verge of order, people invariably value conduct; when the world is on the verge of chaos, people invariably value talk. When people value conduct, then the trend of the times is to sincerity and genuineness; when people value talk, then the trend of the times is to falsehood and deception.

"When the world is on the verge of order, people invariably value justice; when the world is on the verge of chaos, people value profit. When they value justice, the trend of the times is to be deferential; when they value profit, the trend of the times is to be predatory.

"Those who value conduct invariably get interested in justice; those who value talk invariably get interested in profit. How distant justice and profit are from each other!

"Obviously, talking about something isn't comparable to personally practicing it. And practicing it personally isn't comparable to fulfilling it in the mind. When you talk about something, people can hear it; when you personally act on it, people can see it. When you fulfill it in your mind, spirits apprehend it. If even human intelligence cannot be deceived, how about spiritual intelligence?

"So we know that having nothing to be ashamed of in what we say is not as good as having nothing to be ashamed of in what we do, and having nothing to be ashamed of in what we do is not as good as having nothing to be ashamed of in our thoughts. It is harder to be impeccable in our persons than to be impeccable in our words; it is harder to be impeccable in our minds than to be impeccable in our persons. If we are impeccable in mind, then what difficulty is there?". . . .

The fisherman said to the woodcutter, "Such is the grand scale of strategy and adaptation that none but sages can comprehend it. Only through adaptation do you know the waxing and waning of heaven and earth; only through strategy do you know relative importance in the world.

"'Waxing and waning' refer to opportunity; 'relative importance' refers to business. Times may be prohibitive or stable, business may bring loss or gain. If leaders don't know how to negotiate the vagaries of prohibitive and stable times, how can they know what adaptation can accomplish? If leaders don't know how to negotiate the vagaries of opportunities for loss and gain, how can they know what strategy can accomplish?

"Adaptation is working with waxing and waning; strategy is dealing with relative importance. Strategy and adaptation are included in the science of leadership."

The fisherman asked the woodcutter, "Is there any end to petty people?"

The woodcutter said, "No. Princely people are born with positive, balanced mentalities, while petty people are born with negative, unbalanced mentalities. Just as positivity doesn't come about but for negativity, if there were no petty people, there would be no princely people.

"However, there is fluctuation therein. When positivity is 60 percent, then negativity is 40 percent. When negativity is 60 percent, then positivity is 40 percent. When negativity and positivity are half-and-half, then each is 50 percent. From this we know that princely people and petty people have their seasons of waxing and waning. In an orderly era, princely people are 60 percent; when princely people are 60 percent, then petty people are 40 percent, and so certainly cannot overwhelm princely people. In a chaotic era, it is the opposite of this.

"When lords act like lords and subjects act like subjects, fathers act like fathers and sons act like sons, elder brothers act like elder brothers and younger brothers act like younger brothers, husbands act like husbands and wives act like wives, this is referred to as everyone being in their places. When lords do not act like lords and ministers do not act like ministers, fathers do not act like fathers and sons do not act like sons, elder brothers do not act like elder brothers and younger brothers do not act like younger brothers, husbands do not act like husbands and wives do not act like wives, this is referred to as everyone being out of place. These derive from the order or chaos of the era, which cause these conditions to be as they are.

"Princely people normally act better than they say, while petty people speak better than they act. So in an orderly time there are many sincere and genuine people, while in a chaotic time there are multitudes of superficial and pretentious people. When the sincere and genuine are in the minority, they can't achieve things; when superficial and pretentious people are in the minority, they can't spoil things. When achievement predominates, the nation thrives; when failure predominates, the nation perishes. Families also prosper or perish for the same reasons.

"What a vast difference there is between those who cause nations and families to thrive and those who cause nations' and families' demise!"

The woodcutter asked the fisherman, "What people call talent has both benefit and harm—how is that?"

The fisherman said, "Talent is one thing, benefit and harm diverge. There are those whose talents are balanced, and those whose talents are unbalanced. Those whose talents are balanced benefit other people, and this extends to themselves. Those whose talents are imbalanced benefit themselves but harm others in the process."

The woodcutter asked, "If it's unbalanced, how can you call it talent?"

The fisherman said, "If someone can do what others cannot, how can you not call that talent? The reason that sages regret the difficulty of talent is that those who can accomplish the work of the world and balance it are rare. If one cannot restore balance, his talent may be talent, but it would be hard to speak of his humanity.

"For example, it is like medicine treating disease; sometimes toxic medicine is also used. It may be used once, but not repeatedly. If the illness remits, the administration of the toxic medicine is immediately stopped. If it is not stopped, then it will kill the person. Ordinary medicines may be used daily, but they cannot cure serious diseases. A toxin that can expel serious illness without harming the patient has always been considered good medicine. The *I Ching* says, 'Great lords have a mandate to found nations and perpetuate families; petty people are not to be employed.' When the times are peaceful and government is stable, it is counterproductive to employ them. The *Classic of Poetry* says, 'The rocks of those mountains may be quarried for jade.' This seems to refer to the talents of small people."

The woodcutter said to the fisherman, "I do understand that the rise and demise of nations, and the imbalance and balance of talents, are matters of destiny; so why not select the people to employ?"

The fisherman said, "It is the ruler who selects his ministers, yet it is the ministers who select their ruler. The intelligent and the ignorant act in accord with their kind. It is inevitable that sagacious rulers will have sagacious ministers, while decadent rulers will have decadent ministers. If sagacious ministers live in a decadent society, that is like decadent ministers living in a sagacious society—they will certainly not be employed. Even if they wanted to make trouble or promote prosperity, could they indeed do so?

"What the upper classes like, the lower classes will invariably like, as if reflecting or echoing them. Why would it be necessary to compel or induce them to be that way? If the upper classes like justice, the lower classes will like justice, and the unjust will stay away. If the upper classes are fond of profit, the lower classes will be fond of profit, and those who do not profiteer will stay away. When those who like profit are the majority, the empire wanes day by day; when those who like justice are the majority, the empire flourishes day by day. Flourishing day by day means thriving, waning day by day means perishing. Are thriving and perishing so remote? It's all a matter of what those on top like.

"Indeed, when have petty people ever been absent even in orderly times, and when have princely people ever been absent even in times of chaos? But if they are not employed, how can good or bad be done?"

The woodcutter said, "Good people are always a minority, while people who are not good are always a majority. Eras of order are usually rare, while chaotic times are generally common. How do you know that is so?"

The fisherman said, "By observing it in things—what is not that way? For example, in the case of the food grains, even if you weed them, there will be some that don't sprout; whereas with reeds, they'll grow without any weeding, and even if you tried to get rid of them by weeding, you couldn't. From this I know that the ways of princely people and petty people have their own sources.

"When princely people see good, they rejoice; when they see what is not good, they keep away. When petty people see good, they are jealous of it, and when they see what is not good they are delighted. Good and bad each come from their type. When princely people see good they take to it, and when they see what's not good they avoid it. When petty people see good, they avoid it, and when they see what is not good, they take to it. When princely people see duty, they move; when they see profit, they stay put. When petty people see duty, they stay put, but when they see profit, they move. To move on duty profits others; to move on profit injures others. How far apart helping and harming others are!

"Families and nations are the same in that they thrive when there are always more princely people than petty people, and they perish when there are always more petty people than princely people. Those who leave because of the predominance of princely people are petty people, while those who leave on account of the predominance of petty people are princely people.

"Princely people like enlivening, petty people like killing. When there is preference for life, then society is orderly; when there is a predilection for killing, then society is chaotic. Princely people like justice, while petty people like profit. In an orderly society there is a predilection for justice, while in a chaotic society there is a predilection for profit. The pattern is the same."

When the fisherman was finished talking, the woodcutter said, "I've heard that the sage leader Fu Xi lived in antiquity; today I feel like I've met him face-to-face!"

THE MAN OF DEER GATE
A Letter from Retirement
Pi Rixiu

A drunken scholar retired to Deer Gate. When he wasn't drunk, he roamed around; when he wasn't roaming around, he rested. Retiring to the Way, he thought of what he hadn't accomplished; retiring to literature, he was embarrassed by what he hadn't gotten around to. So in response, he wrote letters from retirement. The sage kings of old were able to find the good people among the inhabitants of the mountains and valleys; his intention may have lay in this.

Some say that in Confucius's edition of the *Spring and Autumn Annals,* records of disasters and anomalies are close to superstition, stories of military valor are close to power, governments of deteriorating states are close to chaos, and establishment of rites of propitiation and sacrifice is close to the supernatural, making the Way of rulers fragmented and difficult to enunciate. Are there any unspoken meanings?[1]

In reply it may be said that it would truly be unbelievable for mountains to howl, ghosts to cry, the sky to split, and the earth to break down; what the sage meant is that the oppression of the ruler alone brings on disasters throughout sky and earth, so it is to be avoided, that's all. Even so, there were rulers of later ages who caused disasters by being extremely evil, manifestly aberrant in their absolute oppression.

When there were tyrannical rulers who could "straighten iron hooks with their hands, move pillars by pushing beams, take on bears

---

1. According to the *Analects,* Confucius did not speak of superstition, power, chaos, or the supernatural.

with their bare hands, and run down tigers and rhinos," it means they were exceptionally strong; the sage [Confucius] obscured this and refrained from speaking of it, fearing they'd abuse people because of their esteem for power and take life in their craving for exploits. Nevertheless, among rulers of later ages there were those who were so fond of wrestling as to neglect government, who took in athletes while overlooking savants.

There were cases of adultery and incest, but the sage obscured them and did not speak of them. All that was chaos in the extreme, but the sage obscured it and did not speak of it, fearing that rulers of future generations would become vipers and pigs, and the people would become monsters. Nevertheless, there were those among rulers of later generations who threw states into chaos by wife swapping.

One of the kings of Xia raised dragons for riding, one of the kings of Zhou partied at the Jade Pond. These were quite supernatural indeed, but the sage obscured them and did not discuss them, for fear the rulers of later generations would try to produce things by magic and fulfill their pleasures by sorcery. Nevertheless there were still rulers in later generations who abdicated irresponsibly in search of immortality, or prayed for what they wanted with sacrificial rites.

What a pity! Is it easy to transmit a single word of a sage to guide contemporary society, or a single action that could be a model for the future? In Confucius's time, if he had talked about superstition, power, chaos, or the supernatural, I'm afraid that with rulers of later generations, superstition would not be in goblins and omens, but in government and education; power would not be in wrestling but in invasion and oppression; chaos would not be in their personal life but everywhere in the world; the supernatural would not be in evolution or afterlife, but in clan shrines. So how can it be said that the Way is fragmented?

The effect of education on people is like medicine: taken properly, it affords relief; taken improperly, instead it is harmful.

[9]

HUANG SHI'S SILK TEXT
Zhang Shangying

1. FUNDAMENTALS

The Way, virtue, humaneness, justice, and courtesy—these five are one body.

The Way is what a person treads to cause the great mass of humanity not to know where he's coming from.

Virtue is what a person attains to cause everyone to obtain what they desire.

Humaneness is what a person approaches to have a kind and sympathetic heart, so as to fulfill one's life and development.

Justice is what is good for people, rewarding good and punishing evil, to be successful and constructive.

Courtesy is what people practice, rising early and retiring late, to develop orderly human relations.

Now then, if you wish to be a support for people, you cannot lack even one of these. Savants and noble men understand the courses of waxing and waning, comprehend the factors of success and failure, discern the forces of order and chaos, and master the logic of intelligent choices. Therefore they stay in obscurity, embracing the Way to await their time.

If their time comes and they act on it, they can attain the highest ranks of human service; if they seize the opportune moment to make their moves, they can accomplish unparalleled achievements. Otherwise, if their time never comes, they simply disappear. Therefore their Way is worthy of elevation and their names are respected in later generations.

2. THE RIGHT WAY

Virtue that can embrace the distant, faith that can unite the different, justice that can win the multitude, intelligence that can reflect the ancients, enlightenment that can illumine those below—these are excellent in people.

Conduct that can be a model, wisdom that can resolve objections and doubts, faith that can inspire the keeping of contracts, modesty that can inspire sharing of wealth—these are outstanding in people.

Unremitting diligence, unswerving justice, not trying wrongly to avoid what seems disagreeable, not trying unfairly to obtain what seems profitable—these are exceptional in people.

3. SEEKING ONE'S WILL

To stop addictions and control desires is a means of removing burdens. To suppress wrong and eliminate evil is a means of exorcising error. Abstinence from drinking and carousing is a means of freedom from impurity. Avoiding the objectionable and keeping the doubtful at a distance is a means of not making mistakes. Broad learning and cutting inquiry are means of broadening knowledge.

Lofty conduct and subtle speech are means of cultivating one's person. Respectful restraint and humble modesty are means of self-preservation. Deep calculation and far-reaching consideration are means of not running out of resources. Parental benevolence and friendly directness are means of helping the fallen. Closeness, reciprocity, and earnest conduct are means of dealing with people. Delegating responsibilities according to talent and utilizing abilities are means of getting work done.

Correcting wrongs and prohibiting slander are means of stopping disorder. Considering the past to check the present is a means of avoiding confusion. First measuring, then calculating, is a means of responding to emergencies. Making provisional changes to effect strategy is a means of resolving impasses. Shutting up and conforming is a means of avoiding enmity. Persistence and stubbornness are means of achievement; diligence and conscientiousness are means of guaranteeing the end.

4. MAKING VIRTUE THE BASIS, THE WAY THE SOURCE

In terms of arts of directing the mind and acting with determination, none is superior to comprehensive planning, none is safer than tolerance, none is prior to cultivating virtue, none is more pleasant than a liking for good, none is more spiritual than complete sincerity, none is more enlightened than understanding people and things, none is more auspicious than being content.

Nothing is more painful than having many wishes; nothing is sadder than frittering away of vitality; nothing is sicker than impermanence; nothing is briefer than ill-gotten gain. Nothing is more suffocating than craving what is lowly; nothing is more lonely than being self-centered; nothing is more dangerous than trusting the dubious; nothing is more destructive than too much selfishness.

5. FOLLOWING JUSTICE

Those who try to enlighten the inferior are in the dark. Those who err without realizing it are benighted. Those who stray off and never return are confused. Those who acquire enemies by what they say are cursed. Those who try to command the intractable are abandoned. Those who, by being dilatory, trip up those who have taken initiative are ruined. Those who are not awesome even when angry are defied. Those who like to shame people in public die young. Those who execute or disgrace their delegates are in peril.

Those who slight the respected suffer misfortune. Those who appear to agree when alienated at heart are isolated. Those who are on familiar terms with traitors while distant from the loyal perish. Those who approach beauties while avoiding savants are blind. Those who let their women's private wishes affect their public performance are out of order. Those who give people public offices out of personal preferences are superficial.

Those who look down on subordinates and grab for superiority get attacked. Those whose reputation isn't upheld by reality get worn out. Those who spare themselves while putting the onus on others are undisciplined. Those who are generous with themselves while stingy to others will be abandoned. Those who throw away successes by excesses will lose. Those who are ostracized by their subordinates will sink.

Those who are employing the incompetent will be estranged. Those who give out rewards with an appearance of stinginess will be frustrated. Those who accept a lot but give little will be resented. Those who reject people they've already welcomed will be opposed. Those who give little but expect a lot will not be recompensed. Those who when elevated forget the lowly won't last long. Those who abandon new works because of old grudges will be unfortunate.

Those who employ people improperly are in danger. Those who employ people by force will not prosper. Those who select offices for individuals are out of order. Those who lose their strengths will be weak. Those who determine policy with the inhumane are in peril. Those whose secret plans are leaked outside will fail.

Those who take in a lot and give out but little will wither. Those whose soldiers are impoverished while itinerant orators are rich will decline. Those whose public performance can be bought by bribery are benighted. Those who slight good when they hear of it are crude. Those who never forget mistakes are brutal.

When appointees cannot be trusted, and the trusted cannot be appointed, there is corruption.

Those who govern people with virtue gather; those who rule people with punishments scatter.

If small achievements are not rewarded, great achievements will not be accomplished. If minor resentments are not forgiven, great enmity is sure to develop.

Those whose rewards do not persuade people, and whose penalties are not accepted, will be opposed. Those who reward people who have accomplished nothing, and punish people who have done no crime, are cruel.

Those who like to hear slander of others and hate to hear criticism of themselves will perish.

Those who can keep what they have are secure; those who crave others' possessions will be ruined.

6. MANNERS OF SECURITY

Bitterness is in not giving up minor faults. Trouble is in not planning ahead. Blessings are in accumulating good, curses are in accumulating evil. Famine is in shallow plowing, cold is in lazy weaving. Safety is in winning people, danger is in losing land. Wealth is in meeting what comes, poverty is in rejecting the times.

When those above do not behave consistently, those below have many doubts. Slighting superiors causes offense; look down on those below and you'll have no intimates. If close retainers aren't respectful, distant retainers will slight you. If you doubt yourself, you won't trust others; if you trust yourself, you won't doubt others.

Crooked men have no true friends; devious rulers have no honest subordinates. A state in danger has no wise people; a disorderly administration has no good people.

Those who love humanity deeply seek the wise urgently; those who delight in finding the wise support people cordially.

When a nation is about to become dominant, knights all pledge allegiance; when a country is about to perish, savants are first to flee.

Where the soil is thin, big plants don't grow; where the water is shallow, big fish don't swim. Big birds don't roost in denuded trees; big animals don't dwell in sparse woods.

Mountains that are steep have landslides, wetlands that are filled overflow.

Those who throw away jade and take rock are blind. Those who are like sheep in tiger skin get shamed.

Those whose clothing sags stumble, those who walk without looking at the ground fall.

When the pillars are weak, a house will collapse; when the cabinet is weak, a nation will topple.

When the feet are cold, it hurts the heart; when the people are resentful, it hurts the country.

When the leadership is about to collapse, subordinates crumble first; when a country is about to decline, the people become corrupt first.

When the roots die, the branches wither; when the people are exhausted, the country is ruined.

Those on the same track as an overturned carriage will topple; those who do the same things as a ruined nation will perish.

Seeing what has already occurred, be careful of what is about to happen. If you don't like the aftereffects, avoid them ahead of time. Those who are wary of danger will be safe, those who are wary of destruction will survive.

If people's actions have guidance, they are fortunate; if they have no guidance, they are unfortunate. Good fortune is the resort of a hundred blessings; ill fortune is the target of a hundred curses. That is not supernatural or miraculous, but natural aggregation.

Those who work on good plans have no bad events; those who don't think far ahead will have troubles near at hand.

Those with the same aspiration gain from each other, those with the same humanity worry about each other, those with the same evil gang up with each other, those with the same love seek each other, those with the same beauty are jealous of each other, those with the same knowledge plot against each other, those who prize the same things injure each other, those who seek the same advantages resent each other.

Those with the same voices echo each other, those in the same mood sense each other. Those of the same kind cleave to each other, those with the same principles are friendly to each other. Those who share the same hardships help each other, those on the same path complement each other. Those with the same arts correct each other, those with the same skills strive to outdo each other.

These are results of objective factors and cannot be contravened by theory.

Those who excuse themselves yet direct others are perverse; those who correct themselves and thus influence others are in harmony. What is perverse is hard to follow, what is harmonious is easy to practice. Being hard to follow results in chaos, being easy to practice results in order. In this way it is possible to order oneself, order the home, and order the nation.

WENSHI'S CLASSIC ON REALITY
Officer Xi

1. ONE WORLD

It's not that there is a Way that cannot be spoken; what cannot be spoken is itself the Way. It's not that there is a Way that cannot be conceived; what cannot be conceived is itself the Way.

The phenomena of nature are a raging torrent; human affairs are confused, complicated, and conflicting, contradictory and contentious, a relentless rush, not what they seem to be. And yet they struggle over them, depend on them, spit them up, argue about them, reject them, and demand them.

To speak of it is like spewing shadows, to think of it is like engraving dust. Sage knowledge goes astray, ghosts and spirits do not know. It simply cannot be fabricated, cannot be produced, cannot be measured, cannot be divided, so it is called Heaven, Destiny, Spirit, Mystery; or, combining, called the Way.

Nothing is not Heaven, nothing is not Destiny, nothing is not Spirit, nothing is not Mystery; since things are like this, how could humans be otherwise? All people can be called celestial people, all can be called spiritual people, all can fulfill destiny and comprehend mystery. It cannot be that one is celestial while another is not, or that is destiny while this is not, or that is mystery while this is not. Therefore those who are expert in my Way know heaven, comprehend spirit, fulfill destiny, and reach the mysterious within a single thing. Studying this, you follow up different terms and analyze the same reality; when you get this, you accord with the same reality and forget the different terms.

Looking on the Way is like looking on water: if you think looking at a pond is not enough, you go to a river, or go to the ocean. You say this is the epitome of water, not realizing that your own saliva and tears are both water.

The Way is impersonal; sages do not see one person as affirming the Way and another person as denying the Way. The Way is selfless; sages do not see themselves as having advanced on the Way or regressed in the Way. Because they don't possess the Way, they don't lack the Way; because they don't gain the Way, they don't lose the Way.

Those who do not know the Way and try to figure it out with arbitrary ideas are as if guessing what's under an overturned bowl. If they take it to be of high value, they think of gold or jade. If they take it to be of medium value, they think of horn or feather. If they take it to be of low value, they think of ceramic or stone. Which is right, which is wrong? Only the one who put the object there knows what it is.

One pottery wheel can make myriad vessels, but there is not a single vessel that can make a pottery wheel, or that can destroy a pottery wheel. One Way can make myriad things, but there is no thing that can make the Way or destroy the Way.

The Way, indefinable, seems to have no knowledge; the mind, vacant, seems to have no bonds; things, changing, seem to have no limits.[1] Lightning flashes? Flying sand?[2] Sages thereby know the mind is one, things are one, the Way is one, and the three also combine into one. They do not let unity restrict distinction, and do not let distinction damage unity.

With a bowl for a pond and rocks for islands, fish can swim 'round and 'round there for untold thousands of miles without coming to an end. Why? Because the water doesn't come from anywhere and doesn't go anywhere. The Way of sages originally has no beginning and ultimately has no end, so it can respond to things inexhaustibly.

There is no loving the Way; love is water. There is no contemplating the Way; contemplation is fire. There is no pursuing the Way; pursuit is wood. There is no speaking the Way; speech is metal. There is no thinking of the Way; thought is earth. Only sages ascend the Great

---

1. "Limits" here is used to paraphrase this usage of a character generally employed for negation of identity. "Absence of negation of identity" in this context means that it seems there is nothing that things might not become in the course of change.
2. Lightning flashes and flying sand are images of the transitory and indefinite nature of existence.

Way without leaving their original condition. Since their minds have not sprouted, they are aloof even of the Way.[3]

When layers of clouds cover the sky, and rivers and lakes are dark, the swimming fish are imperceptible. Suddenly, looking up at light on the waves, moving to eat, lucky to receive something from heaven, taking to it, a fish gets hooked and dies. It does not know itself to have no self. Those who chase the Way are also thus.[4]

There are many prescriptions and methods in the world. Some value darkness, some value light; some value strength, some value weakness. If you cling to them, they are all occupations; if you don't cling, they're all the Way.

The Way ultimately cannot be attained; what can be attained is called virtue, it is not called the Way. The Way ultimately cannot be practiced; what can be practiced is called practice, it is not called the Way. Sages use what can be attained and practiced to live well, and use what cannot be attained or practiced to die well.

After hearing the Way, those who contrive anything or cling to anything are relying on the human; those who do not contrive anything or cling to anything are relying on the divine. Whatever is contrived will inevitably fail, and whatever one clings to will inevitably be lost. So "if you hear the Way in the morning, it's all right to die that night."[5]

Obliteration of the whole mental state makes a sage;[6] goodness of the whole mental state makes a savant; badness of the whole mental

---

3. Water, fire, wood, metal, and earth are the so-called five elements or five forces, traditionally used as a fundamental framework for classification and organization of data. The point of this passage distinguishing the Way from individual elements or forces is that all elements are integrated in the Way, while isolated operations of one or another element fragment the experience of the Way. To say that the sage is aloof even of the Way means that the Way is not construed as a mental object.

4. According to commentary, this means that those who get fixated on unusual experiences provoked by trying to practice Taoism are like fish that rise to glimmers of light they've mistaken for food, and thereby get caught.

5. This is a saying of Confucius.

6. This is the equivalent of the Chan Buddhist teaching of "no mind." It does not literally mean oblivion. The Song dynasty master Dahui stipulates, "In Chan terminology, 'mindlessness' does not mean insensitivity or ignorance. It means that the mind is stable and does not get stirred up by the situations and circumstances that one encounters. It means the mind does not grasp anything, it is clear in all situations, unimpeded and undefiled, not dwelling on anything, even nondefilement."

state makes a petty person. Those whose whole mental state is obliterated have gone from being to nonbeing; this cannot be pointed out. Those whose whole mental state is good or bad produce being from nonbeing—this cannot be concealed. Goodness and badness imply having knowledge. All mobile creatures have this. Those whose whole mental state is obliterated are considered to have no knowledge—the Way is everywhere in the world.

Don't think the Way is accomplished by diligence because sages endeavor to practice it tirelessly. Don't think the Way is attained by clinging because sages keep to it firmly, unchanging. Sages' diligent practice is like shooting an arrow—it goes by itself, one does not put it into practice oneself. Sages' firm discipline is like gripping an arrow—it is kept by itself, one does not keep it oneself.

If you seek the Way by sayings or practices, learning or knowledge, you'll toss and turn and never attain. If you realize sayings are like the babbling of a fountain, realize practices are like the flight of a bird, realize learning is like grasping shadows, and realize knowledge is like interpreting dreams, you stop entirely and don't keep them in mind; then the Way will come and accord.

Establishing things for concrete purposes is difficult; eliminating things for the Way is easy. Everything in the world is hard to create and easy to destroy.

One conflagration can burn myriad things; when the things are gone, how can the fire remain? The Way can obliterate myriad things in an instant; when things are gone, where is the Way?

In human life in this world, there are those who live one day and then die, there are those who live ten years and die, there are those who live a hundred years and die. Dying after a day of life is like attaining the Way in an instant; dying after ten years or a hundred years is like taking a long time to attain the Way. Those who have not died can only be called alive, not dead, no matter how they act or appear; those who are not yet in accord with the Way can only be said to be occupied, not on the Way, no matter how they act or appear.

If you do not know my Way has no statement and no practice, and seek the Way from those with mottoes and exercises, if you happen to experience something unusual you will arbitrarily cling to it, considering it the Way, still not realizing that if you abandon the source and pursue the stream you'll never get to the source, and if you abandon the root and take to the branches you'll never get the root.

Learning archery, learning calligraphy, learning the lute, learning chess—there is no occupation that can be grasped instantly. Only the Way, having no form or direction, can therefore be attained in an instant.

When two people shoot together, their relative skill becomes evident. When two people play chess together, winner and loser become evident. But when two people meet on the Way, there is nothing to indicate. "No indication" means there is no cleverness or clumsiness, no winning or losing.

My Way is like the ocean; if a quadrillion gold pieces were thrown in, they'd disappear; if a quadrillion rocks were thrown in, they'd disappear; if a quadrillion pollutants were thrown in, they'd disappear. It can carry tiny shrimp and little minnows, it can carry giant fish and huge whales. It takes in the countless waters combined, without that being too much; and disperses countless waters, distributing them without creating insufficiency.

My Way is like being in the dark: someone in the light can't see anything at all in the dark, but someone in the dark can see even little things distinctly in the light.

The strategy of petty people makes for ill, the strategy of noble people makes for good, the strategy of sages makes for having no object of attainment. Only by having no object of attainment is it called the Way.[7]

My Way is like a sword; if you use the blade to cut things, it's useful, but if you grip the blade with your hand, it will wound you.

The basket doesn't question the beans, and the beans don't answer the basket. The tiles don't question the stones, and the stones don't answer the tiles. If the Way is not lost, is there any question? Is there any answer? One energy circulates—where is the Way?

Those who look to the Way are crawling, those who take to the Way are galloping. Both of them recognize the tasks of the Way but don't know the Way of the Way. Therefore sages do not look toward the Way

---

7. Having no object of attainment, *wusuode* in Chinese, is commonly rendered in Sanskrit as *anupalabdha, anupalabdhi,* and *anupalambha,* which are frequently found in the *Prajnaparamita* and *Vijnanavada* scriptures to refer to the ungraspable nature of absolute truth. In a famous example, the *Vajracchedika-prajnaparamita-sutra* records the Buddha as saying, "There was nothing whatsoever for me to attain in unexcelled complete perfect enlightenment. This is called unexcelled complete perfect enlightenment."

with dissatisfaction and do not rely on the Way to prosper; they do not borrow the Way from sages, and do not sell the Way to fools.

2. TWO PILLARS

Whether a bowl, or a basin, or a vase, or a jug, or a jar, or a dish—all of these can construct omens of heaven and earth. Tortoiseshells, yarrow stalks, broken tiles, patterned rocks—all of these can tell good and bad fortune. So we know that the pattern of creation of sky and earth and myriad things is contained within a single thing, and every thing contains it independently.

When one joins one's own vitality to the vitality of another, the two vitalities stick together and the spirits respond. With one hen and one rooster, eggs are produced; with a male and a female, a fetus is conceived. The form is the vitality of the other, the noumenon is the spirit of the other; the love is one's own vitality, the gaze is one's own spirit. Love is water, gazing is fire. Love clings, and the gaze, based on this, becomes wood. Gaze minds, and love, taking this in, becomes metal. First imagine the energies of a single source complete in one being, hold her and love her to unite with her form, gazing on her with a clear mind to unite with her noumenon. Thus symbols exist therein.[8]

The symbols of the total operation pervade space: ascent from the center is the sky, descent from the center is the earth. There is no ascent without descent, there is no descent without ascent. What ascends is fire, what descends is water; what would ascend but cannot is wood, what would descend but cannot is metal. Wood is such that when you drill it you get fire, when you compress it you get water. Metal is such that when you strike it you get fire, when you melt it you get liquid. Metal and wood are interactions of water and fire: water is vitality, is sky; fire is spirit, is earth; wood is the higher soul, is humanity; metal is the lower soul, is things. What operates endlessly is time; what contains and has location is space. Only earth begins and ends this, and has an explanation of this and an indication of this.

There are countless millions of people in the world; everyone's dreams are different, and every night their dreams are different. There

8. The image of sexual energy used to introduce this segment is interpreted in both literal and metaphorical modes.

are skies, earths, people, things, all composed of thoughts, beyond even the number of atoms. How do we know the present sky and earth are not creatures of thought?

The heart responds to the jujube, the liver responds to the elm; the self responds to sky and earth. When it's going to be cloudy, one dreams of water; when it's going to be sunny, one dreams of fire. Sky and earth commune with the self; the self seems to merge with sky and earth, yet seems to be separate. They're a single whole, yet individual in the end.

Although sky and earth are vast, they have color, they have form, they have measurement, they have location; I have what is not color, not form, not measurement, not location, but makes the sky sky and the earth earth, present.

Those who die in the womb, and those who die in the egg, whether human or animal, certainly do not know the sky and earth, however immense they may be. Whatever measures sky and earth is our limited consciousness. It's like if you don't touch a blade, the blade won't hurt you.

In dreams, in mirrors, in water—there are sky and earth in each of these. Those who want to get away from the sky and earth in dreams don't sleep; those who want to get away from the sky and earth in mirrors don't look in the mirror; those who want to get away from the sky and earth in water don't scoop it in a bowl. The existence or nonexistence of the object is in the subject, not in the object; therefore sages do not leave sky and earth, they detach from consciousness.

The sky is not the sky by itself; there is that which makes it the sky. The earth is not the earth by itself; there is that which makes it the earth. It's like a house, a boat, or a car, which come to be because of people, and do not make themselves. If you know *those* are dependent and know *this*[9] is independent, you do not see the sky above, do not see the earth below, do not see your self within, do not see others outside.

What has time is energy;[10] what is not energy has never had day or night. What has location is form; what is not form has never had south or north.

9. "Those" refers to what is construed; "this" refers to the perceiver.
10. This refers to the fluctuating energies of the day and the night, the lunar cycle, and the four seasons.

What is not energy? The provenience of energy is like waving a fan to get a breeze. Before fanning, it wasn't the energy of the breeze, but once the fanning is going on it is called energy. What is not form? The provenience of form is like drilling wood and getting fire. Before the drilling, it wasn't in the form of fire, but once the drilling is done it's called form.

Changes in cold and heat, warmth and cool, are like the case of tiles and stones, which get hot when put in fire and get cold when placed in water. Huff on them and there's warmth, draw in your breath and there's cool. It's just because external things come and go—the tile and stone really don't have any coming or going. It's like how reflections in water come and go but the so-called water itself really has no coming or going.[11]

When clothes sway in the air, they are getting the energy of the wind. Breathe on something and you get moisture. When water pours into water, it makes a sound; when stone strikes stone, it makes light. Those who know this doctrine can also construct it with wind, rain, thunder, and lightning, because wind, rain, thunder, and lightning are all conditional upon energy, while energy is dependent on mind.[12] It's like if you imagine an immense conflagration inwardly, eventually you'll feel hot, while if you imagine a great flood inwardly, eventually you'll feel cold. Those who know this doctrine can assimilate to all the qualities of sky and earth.

By changes in the five kinds of clouds[13] it is possible to predict how good the year's harvest will be; by the directions of the eight winds[14] it is possible to predict the good and bad fortune of the times. So we know that permission and prohibition, disasters and blessings, are but operations of a single energy. It merges others and self, and equalizes

---

11. This corresponds to the Buddhist idea of *tathata* or "suchness" conceived as a sort of permanent substrate underlying transitory existences.

12. In one of the most famous of popular Chan Buddhist stories, an enlightened layman came upon two monks arguing about a pennant flapping in the wind. One monk argued that the wind was moving, the other monk argued that the pennant was moving. The layman interrupted and said, "It's not the wind, and not the flag—it's your minds moving." This layman later became the celebrated Sixth Patriarch of Chan Buddhism.

13. The five kinds of clouds referred to in this context are classified as blue, white, red, black, and yellow.

14. The eight winds are gain and loss, blame and praise, honor and defamation, pain and pleasure.

heaven and earth, yet the subjective intellect limits it to what is recognized.

Sky and earth temporarily lodge, myriad things temporarily lodge, the self temporarily lodges, the Way temporarily lodges. Without a temporary lodge, even the Way could not be established.

3. THE THREE POLES

The way sages govern the world is not to be intelligent or ignorant themselves, but to take people to be intelligent based on their intelligence, and take people as ignorant based on their ignorance. They do not do right or wrong themselves, but affirm what is right in the course of events and repudiate what is wrong in the course of events.

They know the general similarity of past and present, so they may sometimes give precedence to the ancient and they may sometimes give precedence to the modern. They know the general similarity of inside and outside, so they may sometimes give precedence to the inside and they may sometimes give precedence to the outside.

The things of the world cannot burden them, so they get to their roots by humility; the things of the world cannot estrange them, so they take them in by emptiness. The things of the world cannot cause them difficulty, so they manage them with ease. The things of the world cannot impede them, so they change them by strategy.

By using this to balance the world, it was possible to design manners. By using this to harmonize the world, it was possible to compose music. By using this to be fair to the world, it was possible to order the economy. By using this to reach the whole world, it was possible to prevent contempt. By using this to adapt to the world, it was possible to establish laws. By using this to observe the world, it was possible to design implements.

Sages did not govern the world by themselves; they governed the world by the world. The world attributed the merit to the sages, while the sages left the merit to the world. That is why when Yao and Shun and Yu and Tang[15] governed the land, everyone in the land thought order was spontaneous.

---

15. Yao (trad. r. ca. 2357–2257 B.C.E.), Shun (trad. r. ca. 2255–2207 B.C.E.), Yu (trad. r. ca. 2205–2197 B.C.E.), and Tang (trad. r. ca. 1766–1753 B.C.E.) were idealized rulers of ancient times.

There is nothing the sky doesn't cover; there is life giving and there is killing, but the sky has no love or hate. There is nothing the sun doesn't shine on: there is beauty and there is ugliness, but the sun is neither friendly nor unfriendly.

The Way of sages is divinely ordained; it's not that sages can guide themselves. The virtue of sages is to suit the times; it's not that sages can be virtuous of themselves. The occupation of sages is not to contrive; it's not that sages can occupy themselves. Therefore sages do not possess the Way, do not possess virtue, do not possess work.

Sages know selves have no self, so they treat them as equals with humaneness. They know affairs have no self, so they manage them with justice. They know the mind has no self, so they discipline it with courtesy. They know consciousness has no self, so they watch it with wisdom. They know that words have no self, so they keep them with faithfulness.

The Way of sages may use humaneness for humaneness, or may use justice for humaneness, or may use courtesy, or wisdom, or faithfulness for humaneness. Humanity, justice, courtesy, wisdom, and faithfulness each contain all five; sages unite them without mix-up. The world cannot name this.

Don't view sages in terms of conduct; the Way has no tracks. Don't view sages in terms of speech; the Way has no words. Don't view sages in terms of ability; the Way does nothing. Don't view sages in terms of appearances; the Way has no form.

Even if conduct is utterly outstanding, it is not beyond high and low. Even if speech is completely impartial, it is not beyond right and wrong. Even if ability is sheer genius, it is not beyond skill and ineptitude. Even if the appearance is utterly exceptional, it is not beyond fine and ugly. Sages borrow these to show the world; when the world is blind to them, then it sees the sages.[16]

Sages learned from bees to establish lord and subject; they learned from spiders to make nets; they learned from palm-joining ferrets to design manners; they learned from fighting ants to set up armies. Common people learn from savants, savants learn from sages, sages

16. Cf. *Vajracchedika-prajnaparamita-sutra:* "All appearances are illusory; if you see that appearances are not characteristics, then you see the Tathagata [Buddha]." The citation of pairs of opposites is to indicate the relative or comparative status of any qualification.

learn from all things. Only sages identify with things, so they have no self.[17]

Sages speak of the Way. They observe sky, earth, people, and things; "all are my Way." They advocate and harmonize with it, start and finish it, see it through the seasons, nurture and develop it. They do not love the Way or abandon things, do not revere rulers or despise common people.

Savants speak of things. Things are not the same; day after day they dispense with them, day after day they deal with them, shortening them, lengthening them, straightening them, correcting them. This is being changed by things. What they do not yet know is that whether sages mix in with the vulgar or live separately apart, it is for the sake of others, not for themselves.

Sages are the same as ordinary people in eating and drinking and wearing clothes, the same in their houses, boats, and cars, the same in being rich and noble or poor and lowly. Ordinary people being the same as sages, and sages being the same as ordinary people, what about those who rely on their high status and make much of their greatness—are they that way, or not?

If a fish wants to be different from the other fish and so leaps out of the water onto the bank, then it will die. If a tiger wants to be different from the other tigers and so leaves the mountains to go to the city, it will be captured. Sages are not different from ordinary people; it's just that things cannot bind them, that's all.

The Way has no doing; what responds to the world by means of the Way is work, not the Way. The Way has no location; what posits the Way in things is things, not the Way. Sages ultimately cannot produce the Way to show people.

Like a bell, so a bell; like a bell, so a drum—sages' speech is like so. Like a car, so a car; like a car, so a boat—sages' conduct is like so. No one can name them, thus they repel the words of the world. No one can know them, thus they refute the knowledge of the world.

A centipede eats a snake, a snake eats a frog, a frog eats a centipede—they eat each other. So it is with the statements of sages—they speak of the fallacies of "existence" and "nonexistence," they

---

17. The *Baozanglun* by Sengzhao (384–414), a famous Chinese Buddhist regarded as a pioneer of the doctrine of sudden enlightenment, says, "Sages have no self, but there is nothing that is not their self."

also speak of the fallacies of "neither existence nor nonexistence," and they also speak of the fallacies of repudiating "neither existence nor nonexistence." They speak of these like sawing, so only the expert sages do not leave a single word.

Whether a dragon, a sea monster, a serpent, a turtle, a fish, or a clam, a dragon can be any of these, while a monster can only be a monster, and cannot be a dragon, or a serpent, or a turtle, or a fish, or a clam. Sages act like dragons, savants act like monsters.

When there is no dwelling in yourself, things with form are spontaneously clear. In movement like water, in stillness like a mirror, responding like an echo, subtle as nothingness, silent as clarity, harmonizing with those who are the same, forgetting those who attain, you never presume to precede others but always follow others.

Undifferentiated, unbounded—traveling to the universal beginning, sometimes gold, sometimes jade, sometimes dung, sometimes earth, sometimes a flying creature, sometimes a running creature, sometimes a mountain creature, sometimes a sea creature—is this being direct, or strategic? Crazy, or stupid?

If people are skilled at the harp, when they are sad, their music is sorrowful; when they have longings, their music is slow; when they are resentful, their music is harsh; when they feel yearning, their music is meandering. But the reason for their sorrow, longing, resentment, or yearning is not hands, not bamboo, not strings, not wood. What is found in the heart is matched in the hands; what is found in the hands is matched in things. In people who have the Way, everything conforms to the Way.

Sages are the same as other people in having speech, action, and thought; they are different from other people in never having spoken, acted, or thought.

When consciousness of gain and loss is dominant, relatives don't get along. When consciousness of judgment is dominant, affairs don't turn out for the best. When consciousness of repulsion is dominant, things don't match up. Therefore sages diffuse these.

The ignorant and incompetent of the world give aid incorrectly; the ignorant and incompetent among sages liberate themselves. What is hardly realized is that sages are sometimes ignorant, sometimes enlightened, sometimes clumsy, and sometimes skillful.

A sage who takes a sage for a teacher is a savant; a savant who takes a sage for a teacher is a sage. This is because a sage who takes a

sage for a teacher is following tracks, forgetting the Way, while a savant who takes a sage for a teacher turns away from tracks to unite
with the Way.

Savants head upward and don't see below; common people head
downward and don't see above; sages comprehend both above and below. It's just that they harmonize with them; how could this imply
there are no sages apart from savants and ordinary people?

It is a universal principle that the husband leads and the wife coop-
erates; when the stallion runs, the mare follows; when the cock crows,
the hen responds. On this basis sages regulate speech and conduct,
whereas savants restrict them.[18]

Though the Way of sages may change its stripes, work still plods
along. Though the Way be confusing, work is orderly.

What is called the Way of sages is indescribably unique, indescribably pervasive, indescribably immense, indescribably recondite. Simply
because it can match everything everywhere while nothing whatsoever
can match it, therefore its potential is more valuable than anything.

The wrapping up and rolling out of the clouds, the flight of the birds,
all take place in the open sky, and so they can change endlessly. The
Way of sages too is like this.

4. Four Tallies

Water can be divided up and can be combined; vitality has no person.
Fire can burn on oil and on kindling; spirit has no self.

So even though the ears be covered they can hear before and after,
impersonally; wisdom is noble, impersonally; the number one is odd,
impersonally; winter freezes autumn growth, impersonally; black is
unchangeable, impersonally; north is associated with long life, impersonally. All of this is vitality.

As the tongue touches the lips to articulate words, there is no self;
in courtesy and humility there is no self; in the evenness of the number two there is no self; in summer depending on the growth of spring
there is no self; in the changeability of the color red there is no self; in
the association of the south with early death there is no self. All of
this is spirit.

---

18. According to a Chan saying, "If the law were fully applied, there would be no
people."

As vitality is impersonal, when rice is removed from the husk the vital part remains; as spirit is selfless, when a soul occupies a being then spirit appears.

Those who keep their vitality whole forget affirmation and negation, forget gain and loss; for what is within them is not that. Those who embrace the spirit are obscure or clear according to the time, strong or weak according to the time; what is there is not here.[19]

Vitality and spirit are water and fire. The five elements mutually produce and destroy one another, their coming without beginning and their going without end. So our vitality is a single drop that neither remains in existence nor passes away; our spirit is a single flash with no origin or extinction. By having no self and no person, no beginning and no end, it is possible to merge with sky and earth.

Vitality is water, the lower soul is metal, the spirit is fire, the higher soul is wood. Vitality's indicator is water, the lower soul's indicator is metal; as metal produces water, vitality is stored in the lower soul. Spirit's indicator is fire, the higher soul's indicator is wood; as wood produces fire, the spirit is stored in the higher soul.

Fire can melt metal down and burn wood up; by this means it obliterates the lower and higher souls.[20]

In the sky, vitality is coldness; on earth, it is water; in humans, it is vitality.[21] In the sky, spirit is heat; on earth, it is fire; in humans, it is the spirit. In the sky, the lower soul is dryness; on earth, it is metal; in humans, it is the lower soul. In the sky, the higher soul is wind; on earth, it is wood; in humans, it is the higher soul.

Let us merge our vitality with the vitalities of sky, earth, and all things, just as myriad bodies of water can merge into one body of water; merge our spirit with the spirits of sky and earth and all things, just as myriad fires can merge into one fire; merge our lower soul with the lower souls of sky and earth and all things, just as metal can be alloyed with other metals to make one metal; merge our higher soul with the higher souls of sky, earth, and all things, just as wood from different trees can be grafted into one tree. So sky and earth and all things are our vitality, our spirit, our lower soul, our higher soul. What dies? What is born?

19. "There" refers to external conditions; "here" refers to the inner mind or spirit.
20. Thus releasing vitality and spirit.
21. The word for "vitality" also refers to semen.

In the operation of the five elements, based on vitality there is the lower soul; based on the lower soul there is spirit; based on spirit there is intellect; based on intellect there is the higher soul; based on the higher soul there is vitality. The five elements go round and round unceasingly; this is why our artificial minds have streamed and eddied in Creation for countless millions of years, with never an end.

So pits and sprouts have produced each other in countless myriad plants, but however great the sky and earth may be, they cannot cause a pit to sprout in a void. Hens and eggs have produced each other in countless myriad birds, but however marvelous yin and yang may be, they cannot fertilize a hen without a rooster.

Whatever comes up and concerns us, we absorb it all, and in one breath change things into our self. If there are no things, it is not self. These so-called five elements—who can change them?

Ordinary people who absorb the lower soul with the higher soul have an excess of metal and thus an insufficiency of wood. Sages who convey the higher soul with the lower soul have an excess of wood and thus an insufficiency of metal. That is because when the higher soul contains the lower soul, it accompanies it; while when the lower soul transports the higher soul, it motivates it.

The lower soul lodges in the eyes during the day, the higher soul lodges in the liver at night. What lodges in the eyes sees, what lodges in the liver dreams. That which sees, the lower soul, has no discrimination to analyze; what discriminates and analyzes objects into celestial and earthly is a habit of the lower soul. That which dreams, the higher soul, has no discrimination to analyze; what discriminates and analyzes into other and self is a habit of the higher soul.

As earth produces metal, intellect produces the higher soul. What is moved by spirit is not called spirit, but is called intellect.[22] What is moved by intellect is not called intellect, but is called the higher soul. Only sages know that selves have no self, things have no entity, and all

22. The Chinese character rendered "intellect" here has a number of meanings applying to mind and mental functions, as does the character generally rendered "mind." The former is used to translate the Sanskrit word *manas*, the latter is used to translate the Sanskrit word *citta*. In both Chinese and Sanskrit languages there is a fundamental range of overlap, with some scope for differentiated usage. Because English also has general and specific usages that cannot be aligned, arranged, or evoked all at once, there is no way to create a standard system of terminology that can obviate all formal redundancies or apply to all conceptual contexts.

exist based on thought construing them.[23] Therefore when myriad things come, I respond to them all by nature and do not respond to them by mind. In nature, mind hasn't sprouted. With no mind, there is no ideation, as when there's no earth without fire. Without ideation, there's no higher soul, as there is no metal without earth. If one is not there, all five disappear.

Once you merge sky and earth and all things into the lower soul, then you can merge sky and earth and all things into the higher soul: what is beautiful in Creation is our lower soul, what exists in Creation is our higher soul; then there is nothing at all that can compel us.

Soul that's cloudy is the lower soul, soul that's clear is the higher soul. This is in accord with the ideograms.[24] Soul is what becomes of a person after death, clouds are associated with wind, and wind is associated with wood. Clarity is associated with energy, and energy is associated with metal.

Wind disperses, so it is light and pure; what is light and clear rises to the sky. Metal is hard, so it is heavy and opaque; what is heavy and opaque sinks into the earth. The light and clear is the higher soul rising from the lower soul; the heavy and opaque is the lower soul descending from the higher soul.

There are those who rise through humaneness to become assistants of the wood planet. There are those who rise through justice to become assistants of the metal planet. There are those who rise through courtesy to become assistants of the fire planet. There are those who rise through knowledge to become assistants of the water planet. There are those who rise through faithfulness to become assistants of the earth planet.[25]

There are those who sink through inhumanity, to be ravaged by wood.

23. This is identical to the Buddhist doctrine of *vijnaptimatrata*, that things as we conceive them are not things in themselves but essentially only representations. In the context of China, Korea, and Japan, some confusion of both metaphysical and pragmatic nature has been occasioned by the fact that the Chinese word for Sanskrit *vijnapti*, "representation," and the Chinese word for Sanskrit *vijnana*, "consciousness," are written with the same character *(shi)*.

24. That is, this interpretation is based on the structure of the characters.

25. The wood planet is Jupiter, the metal planet is Venus, the fire planet is Mars, the water planet is Mercury, and the earth planet is Saturn. This passage reflects the idea of a celestial hierarchy of realized people, characteristic of Taoist grotto cults.

There are those who sink through injustice, to be ravaged by metal. There are those who sink through discourtesy, to be ravaged by fire. There are those who sink through ignorance, to be ravaged by water. There are those who sink through unfaithfulness, to be ravaged by earth.

When the lower soul and upper soul are half-and-half, then you are in the human realm. If you elevate your lower soul, you become noble; if you degrade your higher soul, you become base. If you perfect your lower soul, you become wise; if you overstrain your higher soul, you become stupid. If you make your lower soul light, you become enlightened; if you make your higher soul heavy, you become benighted. Raise the lower soul and you become an immortal; dull the higher soul and you become an animal. Illumine the lower soul and you become a spirit; dim the higher soul and you become a ghost.

One's form, one's abode, one's consciousness, and one's predilections all correspond to the five elements. But the proportions of the five elements vary; that is why myriad things are so many as to fill sky and earth, yet still are unending.

Reducing the five phenomena[26] to the five elements, and making the five animals[27] from the five elements, can everything be said? It's like auguring from turtle shells, or reckoning from yarrow sticks—with total truthfulness there is spontaneous accord. If the truth of the correspondences of the five elements isn't accurate, then you'll never augur or calculate correctly. Sages make temporary use of things to get around in the world; the five elements have to apply.

Five[28] all contain the lower soul. The lower soul contains consciousness, the eyes contain vitality, the body contains spirit. What sees them is the lower soul; the ears, eyes, mouth, nose, and mind are like this.[29]

The creative agent in the subject is love, which makes vitality, which constitutes the father-root of birth of the other. Contemplation is the mother-root of the birth of the other. Although love and

---

26. The aforementioned vitality, spirit, intellect, upper soul, and lower soul.
27. The five animals refer to the multitude of animals in terms of the five natural garbs of feathers, fur, shell, scales, and naked skin.
28. Commentary refers to eyes, ears, nose, mouth, and mind as the five faculties; sound, form, scent, flavor, and phenomena as the five objects; and seeing, hearing, smelling, tasting, and thinking as the five consciousnesses.
29. Taking *zhi lei* to intend *lei zhi*.

contemplation are different, they're both based on consciousness; their creation of life is essentially always there.

As the creative agent is one, the father, so we receive energy from our father, which makes water. Two is the mother, so we receive blood from our mother, which makes fire. With father and mother, reproduction goes on. But if love has no consciousness, like the light of a lamp, self-consciousness doesn't sprout, so how can the creation of ego take place?

It's like a drumstick beating a drum: the form of the drumstick is our existence, the sound of the drum is our responsiveness. After the drumstick is gone, sound still reverberates, but in the end no longer remains. The form of the drumstick is like our vitality, the sound of the drum is like our spirit; the reverberating sound is like the lower soul and higher soul. If you know they come and go suddenly, what are the energies of the five elements to you?

For fruit to have pits requires the presence of water, fire [warmth], and earth all together; then they can reproduce endlessly. If all three are not present, it's like a drought, a flood, or a massive clod, none of which can grow anything. Now, the water of vitality, the fire of spirit, and the earth of intellect originally do not mix; only because people join them at the roots is it possible to have the illusions of perceiving the existence of phenomena therein, just as enchanters can produce perceptions of many things where there is nothing at all.

The lower soul is wood; trees root in the water of winter and flower in the fire of summer, so humans' lower soul is stored in the vitality of the night and appears in the spirit of the day. When it combines with vitality, what is seen is individual to oneself, because vitality has no other; when it combines with spirit, what is seen is common to others, because spirit has no self.

One who knows that the body is like the body in dreams, appearing according to the mental state, can thereby cause the spirit to fly as the self, roaming the empyrean sky. One who knows that things are like things in dreams, appearing according to the mental state, can congeal vitality into things and ride the eight directions.

This Way makes it possible to perceive vitality and spirit, and so prolong life; and makes it possible to forget vitality and spirit, and so transcend life.

Inhaling energy to nourish vitality is like metal producing water; inhaling air to nourish spirit is like wood producing fire.[30] This is how to borrow the external to enhance vitality and spirit. Swallowing saliva to nourish vitality so that vitality is not exhausted,[31] and warming by massage to nourish the spirit so that spirit is not exhausted, are ways of borrowing the internal to enhance vitality and spirit.[32]

As for forgetting vitality and spirit to transcend life, this is the Way. I have already spoken of it.

When a person is conscientiously courteous, the spirit does not race outside; it is thereby possible to concentrate the spirit. When a person is conscientiously wise, vitality does not shift outside; it is thereby possible to control vitality. Humaneness is positive and illuminating; it is thereby possible to lighten the lower soul. Duty is dark and invisible; it is thereby possible to govern the higher soul.

A dung beetle rolls dung into a ball; when the ball is complete, the beetle concentrates on it, and there are maggots in the ball, which soon molt. If the beetle didn't concentrate, how could the maggots appear?

A cook makes soup of a crab, leaving one leg on the cutting board. The crab is already soup, yet the leftover leg is still wriggling. This is because life and death are just the concentration and dispersal of one energy; it is not born and does not die, but people subjectively construe it as being born and dying.

There are those who die standing, there are those who die sitting, there are those who die lying down. There are those who die of desires, and there are those who die of drugs. They're equally dead, with no difference between A and B. People who know the Way don't see birth, so they don't see death.

For people to reject birth and death, or transcend birth and death, are both tremendous troubles. It's like the case of a phantom; if one has an attitude rejecting birth and death, or an aspiration to transcend birth and death, one can only be called a spook—this is not called the Way.

Among those who conceive of birth and death, some say there is existence after death, some say there is nonexistence after death, some say there is both existence and nonexistence after death, some say there is neither existence nor nonexistence after death. Some say

30. This distinction refers to the physical and mental aspects of breathing exercises.
31. Production of saliva, an important element in Taoist health lore, commonly decreases in seniors. This can lead to insufficient appetite and imperfect digestion.
32. Tension and relaxation of the body affect mood and attention.

it is to be welcomed, some say it is to be feared. Some say it should be let be, some say it should be transcended. Changing their consciousness and feelings more and more, they run wild, unceasing, not realizing that the birth and death of the self are like the hands of a horse, or the wings of an ox—they have never existed, and don't even have any nonexistence. It's like water and fire; even in contact, fire can't burn fire, and water can't drown water.

5. FIVE MIRRORS

Those whose minds are corrupted by fortune-telling are taken in by the demon of the supernatural. Those whose minds are corrupted by sexuality are taken in by the demon of debauchery. Those whose minds are corrupted by hidden worries are taken in by the demon of depression. Those whose minds are corrupted by heedlessness are taken in by the demon of sociopathy. Those who are corrupted by compacts with deities are taken in by the demon of miracles. Those who are corrupted by medicines and diet are taken in by the demon of material objects.

Such demons may have negative energy for a body, or may have darkness for a body, or may have air for a body, or may have energy for a body, or may have a clay image for a body, or may have a painted picture for a body, or may have a broken vessel for a body. The other, with its vitality, and the subject, with its vitality, combine vitalities and the spirit responds. Those who are taken in by a demon may become capable of wonders, or oddities, or auspicious phenomena; in their conceit those people don't say a demon is in them, they only say the Way is in them. Eventually some die on wood, some die of metal, some die in rope, some die in wells.

Only sages can sublimate spirit rather than consider spirits sacred. Employing all things and keeping hold on their mechanisms, they can combine them, they can disperse them, and they can inhibit them. They respond to myriad things every day, but their minds remain calm.

Without a unified mind, as the five consciousnesses[33] all run the mind cannot be unified. Without an empty mind, as the five elements

---

33. The basic sense consciousnesses, the consciousnesses of seeing, hearing, feeling, smell, and taste.

are all present the mind cannot be emptied. Without a quiet mind, as myriad changes minutely move the mind cannot be quieted.

If you are capable of unity, then duality will match it; if you are capable of emptiness, then solidity will fill it; if you are capable of quiet, then activity will stir it. Only sages can absorb all that exists in one breath, so nothing can enslave their intelligence; and thoroughly disperse one breath into all that exists, so nothing can impede their activities.

A flame that's been burning for a thousand years can go out in an instant; a thousand years' consciousness can go out in an instant.

What floats is the boat; what floats it is the water, not the boat. What runs is the cart; what makes it go is the ox, not the cart. What thinks is the mind; what enables thought is the intellect, not the mind.[34] No one knows why it's so, but it is. Since it is so without anyone knowing why, it comes from nowhere and goes no place. Therefore it can provide the universe with a basis, fundamentally not of the past or the present.

If you know there's nothing to the mind, then you realize there's nothing to things. When you know there's nothing to things, then you know there's nothing to the Way. Because you know there's nothing to the Way, you do not revere exceptional behavior and are not startled by subtle words.

When objects and self interact, mind is produced; when two pieces of wood rub together, fire is produced. You cannot say this is in the self, nor can you say it is in the other; yet you cannot say it is not self, and cannot say it is not other. If you fixate on it as other or self you're ignorant.

There's no relying on what you call gain and loss and right and wrong. What you call gain and loss and right and wrong, can you actually consider gain or loss or right or wrong? Even sages don't know, much less you![35]

A dream at night may be longer than a night; the mind has no time. If someone is born in Qi, everything his mind sees is of the state of Qi. Once he goes to Song, to Wei, to Liang, to Jin, what is present to his mind is in each case different; the mind has no place.

A good archer takes the bow for a teacher, not a model archer; a

---

34. In Buddhist terms, this would refer to the distinction between the *manas* and the *alayavijnana.*

35. This refers to the contextual and perceptual variability of such evaluations.

good boatman takes the boat for a teacher, not a model boatman; one with a good mind takes the mind for a teacher, not sages.

Right and wrong, fine and ugly, success and failure, filling and emptying—that which creates things runs these. All exist due to subjective consciousness clinging to them. Now if you use nonexistence to dismiss them, this is still there; use neither-existence-nor-nonexistence to dismiss that, and this is still there. Nonexistence means silence, nonexistence means indistinctness; still being there is like going back to a place you've been in the past and finding it just as you remembered it. This cannot be forgotten, cannot be dismissed.[36]

Those who are good at detachment from perception turn perception into knowledge. Do you know the teacher of turning perception into knowledge? "Imagination" is like getting frightened when you think of ghosts, or getting fearful when you think of robbers; "perception" is like taking glutinous millet for nonglutinous millet, like taking jade for rock. Both are superficial, unstable, indefinite, not grounded anywhere. It's like when you see something odd you conceive the mental image of something odd and produce the perception of something odd. This mental image, this perception, is not originally in the self.[37]

For example, today is only today; tomorrow's mental images and perceptions will be different, unpredictably. When tomorrow comes, the welter of thoughts and perceptions will all arise in connection

36. This sort of dialectic is found in various forms of Mahayana Buddhist meditation. See, for example, *Cessation and Contemplation in the Five Teachings of the Hua Yen* by Du Shun, particularly section 5, *Flower Ornament Meditation*, translated in *Classics of Buddhism and Zen* by Thomas Cleary, volume 5, pp. 590–593.

37. The word for "imagination" or "mental image" is conventionally used in Buddhist texts to translate Sanskrit *samjna*, cognate to cognition, and used to mean conception, which Buddhist usage designates a mental construction. The Taoist usage here follows the Buddhist usage in the sense that it emphasizes the constructed nature of the mental phenomenon in question. As a verb, the character here translated as perception means knowing or representing, depending on context; as a noun it means consciousness, conventionally used in Buddhist texts to translate *vijnana*, but in the conceptual framework of Buddhist analysis, consciousness is associated with the faculties or organs of sense, so that the sense-consciousnesses, which in Buddhism include cognitive consciousness as a sixth sense, are examined as discrete *dhatu*, or "elements," alone and in combination with other elements. In English it is awkward to speak of so many consciousnesses occurring in an individual in the course of a day, so the translation resorts to the associated sense of perception, which implies a formation of consciousness and is readily recognized as multiple and changing.

with what's there. To call this "thought and perception" is like the example of the rhinoceros looking up at the moon, such that the shape of the moon [seems to] nestle in the [curve of] the rhino's horn. This only occurs in perception; the real moon is never actually in the horn. So, too, the sky, earth, and myriad things inside the mind. Those who know this doctrine do not see things outside, and do not see mental states inside.

Things are born from earth, and turn into earth in the end. Matters are born from the intellect and turn into ideas in the end. If you know they're only ideas, then as you now affirm them, now deny them, now approve them, now disapprove them, ideas change but the mind doesn't change. The intellect has awareness, while the mind has no awareness, just the single mind of the self; so ideas are like dust that comes and goes, matters are like gusts of wind that arise and die out, while our mind has something vast and eternal existing in it.

Feelings occur in the mind, the mind occurs in nature. Feelings are the ripples, mind is the stream, nature is the water. Whatever happens to us is momentary; if we accept it through nature, then mind will not be aroused and things will be ephemeral.

The smart and the stupid, the genuine and the artificial—there are those who discern, and those who do not discern. While others may be smart or stupid, and others may be genuine or artificial, what calls them smart or stupid or genuine or artificial is tied to our own discernment. If you know they're both creations of consciousness, then even the genuine can be considered artificial.

Mind sensing things doesn't produce mind, it produces feelings. Things interacting with mind doesn't produce things, it produces perceptions. Since things are not real themselves, how much less so perceptions! Since perceptions themselves are not true, how much less so feelings! And yet deluded people grasp the utterly nonexistent and take it to exist, grasp the ever changing and take it to be constant.

Admit one feeling, and it builds up into myriad feelings; admit myriad feelings, and they build up into myriad things. Things come endlessly, while our mind has limits; so our intuition is inhibited by feelings, while our basic feelings are inhibited by things. This can be made to go and can be made to come, but the going and coming have never been up to us—Creation causes them, assuring there is no end to it.

What is yet to be realized is that however immense the sky and earth may be, they can only compel what has form, and cannot compel what has no form. However marvelous yin and yang, they can only compel what has energy and cannot compel what has no energy. Where mind goes, energy follows it; where energy goes, form responds to it. It is like the way space inside one energy transmutes it into myriad things, but the energy is not called space. Our one mind can turn into energy and can turn into form, yet our mind has no energy and no form. If you know your own one mind has no energy and no form, then sky and earth and yin and yang cannot compel you.

When people are in a normal condition and their eyes suddenly see something unusual, in every case there is a crystallization of vitality that makes it so. When people are ill and their eyes suddenly see something unusual, in every case there is a dissatisfaction of the heart that makes it so. If you know your own mind can cause the nonexistent to appear to exist, then you know your own mind can cause the existent to seem nonexistent. Just don't believe in it, and it naturally won't be baffling.

It may be said, since this consciousness is already benighted, who is capable of disbelief? I say it is like the way a snake catcher doesn't fear snakes; even though he dreams of snakes, he's not frightened. Therefore the Yellow Emperor said, "There are no ghosts or spirits on the Way—one goes alone and comes alone."

Our thoughts change every day. There is something that compels this that is not self, but destiny. If you know it is only destiny, you do not see self outside and do not see mind inside.

As the eyes gaze upon the carved and polished, their clarity is increasingly impaired. As the ears listen to concert music, their clarity is increasingly impaired. As the mind thinks of mystery and marvel, the mind is increasingly impaired.

Don't try to figure out others by your own mind, try to figure them out by their minds. Those who know how to do this can thereby manage affairs, can thereby practice virtue, can thereby consistently keep to the Way, can thereby socialize with others, can thereby forget self.

It is a universal pattern that if small things aren't controlled they get big, and if big things aren't controlled they get unmanageable. So those who can control a state of mind can thereby develop virtue; those who can forget a state of mind can thereby conform to the Way.

6. SIX TRANSFORMATIONS

People of the world who divide others and self because their own thoughts differ from others' thoughts, and others' thoughts differ from their own thoughts, still do not realize that people in dreams also differ from others in their thoughts, and others differ from them in their thoughts, so who is self, who is other? Those who divide others and self because their own pains differ from others' pains, and others' pains differ from their own pains, still don't realize that people in dreams also differ from others in their pains, and others differ from them in their pains, so who is self, who is other?

Nails and hair don't feel pain, hands and feet don't think, and yet they are also us—how can we be considered different by reason of thought or pain? People of the world consider individual perception to be dreaming, and consider perception in common to be wakefulness. They still don't realize that as a crystallization of vitality, a person may also perceive individually in daytime, while as a meeting of spirits, two people may have the same dream at night. Both are our own vitality and spirit, so which is dreaming, which is waking?

People of the world take temporary perceptions to be dreaming, and take enduring perceptions to be waking. They still don't realize that temporary perceptions are yin and yang energy, and enduring perceptions are also yin and yang energy. Both are our own yin and yang, so which is dreaming, which is waking?

People who like humaneness often dream of pine and cedar, peach and plum. Those who like justice often dream of weapons and irons. Those who like ritual often dream of ceremonial vessels. Those who like wisdom often dream of rivers, lakes, and wetlands. Those who like faithfulness often dream of mountains and plains. This is invariably so of anyone compelled by the five elements, but it may happen that one hears something in a dream, or thinks something, and the dream changes accordingly, not subject to the control of the five elements. Sages govern things by mind, and control mind by nature, so their minds merge with Creation, and the five elements cannot constrain them.

If you see someone with a snake's head and a human body, or with an ox's arms and fish scales, or with a demon's form and a bird's wings, don't think them weird. These monsters are not as weird as dreams, and dreams aren't as weird as waking, with ears, eyes, hands, and arms, their weirdness extreme indeed! Great words cannot be spoken, great wisdom cannot be thought.

When people ask me, "What is your clan, what is your surname, what is your name? What is your diet, what is your dress? Who are your friends, who are your servants? What is your music, what is your literature? What is your past, what is your present?" I remain silent and do not answer a single word. If someone keeps after me so I have to respond, I say, "I don't even see 'me'—what can I consider 'mine'?"

Forms can be distinguished and can be combined, can be extended and can be concealed. One woman who's had two husbands can have two children whose features can be distinguished, while when two people, husband and wife, have one child, their features can be combined. Eating black sesame results in long life, so form can be extended. On a moonless night, without fire people cannot even see themselves, so form can be concealed.[38]

Since one energy produces myriad things, even falling hair can be replaced, thus distinguishing forms. Since one energy unites myriad things, even split lips can be mended, thus joining forms. Maintaining energy by spirit, maintaining the body by energy, thus form can be extended. Merging body with spirit, merging spirit with energy, thus form can be concealed. Do you want to know this? Do you want to do this?

If there's nothing that cannot be seen, then there's nothing that is not our seeing. If there's nothing that cannot be heard, then there's nothing that is not our hearing. As five substances can nourish our bodies, nothing is not our body. As the five flavors can nourish our energy, nothing is not our energy. Therefore our body and energy are the universe and all things.

When a tiller is used to oxen, he's rough. When a hunter is used to tigers, he's brave. When a fisher is used to water, he can dive. When a soldier is used to horses, he's sturdy. So all things can become oneself. Within one's own individual body, parasites grow and lice and fleas can infest outside; chapping and chancre are referred to in terms of tortoise

---

38. The word used for "form," while often employed generally in reference to material objects and energetic configurations, here specifically refers to the physical body. This is a common specialization, sometimes meant to be understood within a more general usage, and sometimes, as here, intended as the primary meaning. Even when primarily used in a specialized sense, of course, it may still be extended as an analogy or metaphor.

and fish,[39] scabs are referred to as mice and ants.[40] So all things can become myriad things.

Self being self is like gold in ashes, not like gold in ore or sand. Crush ore and you can get gold, wash sand and you can get gold; but you can toss ashes all your life and you'll never get any gold.

A bee is tiny, but it still can tour sky and earth; a shrimp is tiny, but it still can roam the ocean.

Statues may be of nobles or commoners, men or women, but they're made of earth and disintegrate into earth—are they persons?[41]

When the eyes look at themselves, there is no form; when the ears listen to themselves, there is no sound; when the tongue tastes itself, there is no flavor; when the mind assesses itself, there is no thing.[42] Ordinary people pursue what is outside, savants hold on to the inward; sages consider both artificial.

Our bodies are the energies of the five elements, and the energies of the five elements are one thing, in essence. It is as if in one place you could draw water, obtain fire, grow wood, temper metal, and modify earth. That essence is inclusive, without differentiation, so where feathered creatures abound, furred creatures do not thrive, and where furred creatures abound, feathered creatures do not thrive. Those who know the interactions of the five elements can thereby forget self.

A dead tortoise has no self, yet it can manifest great knowledge.[43] A magnet has no self, yet it can manifest great force. A bell has no self, yet it can manifest a great sound. Boats and carriages have no selves, yet they can manifest distant journeys. So even though our individual body has intelligence, strength, motility, and voice, it has never had a self.

There is a kind of creature that can kill us by shooting our shadows, so we know that what has no knowledge is also self. Therefore self is everywhere in the whole world.

39. Chapped hands are called "tortoise hands," chancre is called "fish mouth."
40. A word for a scabrous condition is written with a character commonly used for "mouse" plus a homonym of a synonym of a character for "ant."
41. According to commentary, this symbolizes the social and psychological creation of status, which as such is not intrinsically real. The object of the exercise is to see the human as a natural entity prior to a social definition.
42. These impossible acts stand for a meditative exercise focusing on consciousness of a sense faculty without a sense object. This is a variation on the technique referred to in Tiantai and Chan schools of Buddhism as "turning the light around and reversing awareness."
43. This refers to the ancient use of tortoiseshells for divination.

One whose mind is wrapped up in thought will even forget hunger; one whose mind is angry will even forget cold. One whose mind is nursed will even forget illness; one whose mind is excited will even forget pain. If you inhale energy to cultivate harmony, what can make you hungry? If you keep mindful of spirit to cultivate warmth, what can make you cold? If you nourish the five organs with the five elements, then they will not be damaged; what can make you ill? If you return the five organs to the five elements, then there is no cognition; what can pain you?

People are not selfless by virtue of ignorance and inaction. Even knowledge and action do not compromise their selflessness. They're like fire, ceaselessly in motion, never having a self.

7. SEVEN CAULDRONS

The Way is basically utterly nonexistent; those who return matters to the Way attain it in one breath. Matters are basically totally existent; those who carry on matters by means of the Way go through it in a hundred actions.

Those who attain the nobility of the Way can assist society thereby. Those who attain the individuality of the Way can establish themselves thereby.

Those who know the Way is not something time can contain are able to make a day into a century and a century into a day. Those who know that the Way is not something space can bound are able to make a mile into a hundred miles and a hundred miles into a mile.

Those who know the Way has no energy but can operate what has energy can thereby summon wind and rain. Those who know the Way has no form but can transmute what has form can thereby change birds and beasts.

Those who attain the clarity of the Way cannot be burdened by anything; their bodies are so light they can ride phoenixes and cranes. Those who attain the wholeness of the Way cannot be submerged by anything; their bodies are so imperceptible they can keep company with monsters.

The existent has no existence, the nonexistent exists—those who know this Way can thereby control ghosts and spirits.

Solidity is empty, emptiness is solid—those who know this Way can penetrate metal and stone.

Above is below, below is above—those who know this Way can attend the stars and planets.

Past is present, present is past—those who know this Way can predict the future.

Others are self, self is others—those who know this Way can see into the lungs and livers of other people.

Things are self, self is things—those who know this Way can develop the dragon and tiger in their guts.[44]

If you know that images come from modifications of mind, by observing in this way, the mind can produce the girl and boy;[45] if you know energy is born from mind, and inhale it in this way, the spirit can become the forge.[46]

Use this to overcome things and you can tame tigers and leopards; use this to assimilate to things and you can enter water and fire. Only those who have the Way are able to do this, and are also able to refrain from doing it even though they can.

Human powers include means of usurping the creativity of sky and earth, like making thunder in winter and ice in summer, enabling corpses to walk and dead trees to bloom, trapping demons in beans and hooking fish in a cup, getting a door in a picture to open, or getting a clay idol to speak. All of those are done by pure energy, which makes it possible to transmute myriad things.

Present conditions do not remain static. They, too, are made by energy, and what energy is like in substance is that it combines and disperses. What enables us to operate energy has never combined or dispersed. What combines is born, what disperses dies; what has never combined or dispersed has no birth and no death. Travelers come and go, but the way station is always like so.

There are those who recite spells, there are those who propitiate deities, there are those who tattoo words, there are those who manipulate their fingers—all of them can compel spirits, control energy, and transmute myriad things. Insincere people find it hard to believe in themselves and easy to believe in things, so they make use of these

---

44. According to commentary, the "dragon and tiger in the gut" refer to the energies of the lower and higher souls.

45. The "girl and boy" refer to yin and yang energies.

46. This refers to keeping attention on the breathing. This exercise is used to foster concentration that can be used for purifying the mind and for creative visualization; hence the metaphor of the forge.

techniques to perform these feats. If they knew, sincerity alone has the wherewithal for this without depending on another.

People's exhalation and inhalation travels four hundred thousand *li* a day; changes can be said to be rapid indeed! Only a sage does not mind and is not altered.

Master Blue Phoenix lived for a thousand years, and passed on at the age of a thousand; Master Peach served in office five times and his mind changed five times. Sages are guests of affairs, detached from things, yet hardly disdaining to be constructive in society. Those who are subject to the determinants of physical embodiment fear unknowability of changes.

As myriad things change and evolve, though they may alternately disappear and appear, energy is one and only one. Only sages know the one and aren't changed.

The growth of nails and hair and the circulation of nutrients never cease for a moment; ordinary people see this when it has become obvious, but they can't see it happening subtly. Sages let change be, so they do not change.

In your room is what you normally see and hear; once you go to the door, go to the neighbors, go to the village, go to the club, once you go to the countryside, go to the mountains, go to the riverside, what you see and hear differs in each setting, but your likes and dislikes go along with you, accord and contention follow you, gain and loss mold you. Therefore sages have discipline in their conduct.

Just as the ocean produces millions of fish yet the water is but one, we are together with a profuse proliferation of beings within universal evolution, yet our essential nature is but one. For those who know the oneness of essential nature, there is no person, no self, no death, no birth.

It is a universal pattern that right may turn into wrong and wrong may turn into right; gratitude may turn into enmity, and enmity may turn into gratitude. For this reason sages always take change into consideration.

When people are young, they should absorb the lessons of their fathers and elder brothers. When people mature, they should live up to the examples of their friends and companions. When people grow old, they should be heedful of what the youth and adults say. Then, though myriad changes go on, they cannot trouble you.

It is a universal pattern that what is light is easy to change and what is heavy is hard to change. For example, wind and clouds may change and disappear in a moment, while the nature of gold and jade remains unchanged forever. People who are light and clear can evolve along with Creation, not remaining static, and yet with something unchanged remaining.

Two childhood friends don't recognize each other when they're grown up; two who were friends in adulthood don't recognize each other in old age. Like the changes in sparrows and pigeons, hawks and doves, they have no past or present.

8. EIGHT TALLIES

In ancient times, skilled diviners could show the past in the present, show the present in the past, show the low in the high, show the high in the low, show the great in the small, show the small in the great, show the many in the one, show the one in the many, show things in people, show people in things, show other in self, show self in other.

Such is this Way that its coming has no present, its going has no past; it is so high nothing covers it, so low nothing carries it; it is so vast there is no outside, so minute there is no inside. There is no thing outside, no person inside; there is no self at hand, no other at a distance. It cannot be broken down, cannot be cobbled together, cannot be taught, cannot be thought. It is precisely that total integrity that makes it the Way.

Water sinks, so it clusters, forming five crystals. Fire flies, so it travels, producing five odors. Wood grows, so it flowers, making five colors. Metal is hard, so it solidifies, making five sounds. Earth is mellow, so it enriches, producing five flavors. The constants are five in number, their modifications are countless. The materials are five in number, their combinations are countless. So there are myriad things between sky and earth; you cannot grasp them as myriad, you cannot grasp them as five, you cannot grasp them as one. You cannot grasp them as not myriad, you cannot grasp them as not five, you cannot grasp them as not one. You may combine them, or you may separate them, but you thereby require form, proportion, and energy; you just belabor yourself to no avail, that's all—things don't know you and you don't know things.

In our very own minds we can make myriad things. When the mind goes somewhere, love goes along; as love goes along, vitality follows it. When the mind is fixated on something, it first congeals into water. When the mind hankers after something, one drools; when the mind is sad about something, one weeps; when the mind is embarrassed about something, one sweats.

Nothing temporary doesn't continue, nothing that continues doesn't change. Water produces wood, wood produces fire, fire produces earth, earth produces metal, metal produces water. They attack and overcome each other countless times. The young boy and the virgin girl, the gold tower and the crimson chamber, the green dragon and the white tiger, the precious cauldron and the scarlet furnace, all refer to these things.[47] There still exists that which is not these things.[48]

Birds and beasts now cry, now follow, now fly; plants and trees now sprout, now flourish, now fade. Sky and earth cannot stop them, sages cannot tie them down; those that have support survive. But to have this is in the other, not the self; a drum doesn't sound without a drumstick. Pairing is up to the other, individuality is in the self; the drumstick won't beat but for the hand.

They are equally a thing, but ordinary people, confused by their names, see things and do not see the Way. Savants, analyzing the patterns, see the Way and do not see things. Sages, combining them, do not see the Way and do not see things.

Every single thing is the Way. If you don't cling to something, it is the Way; if you cling to it, it is a thing.

Those who know things are artificial don't have to get rid of things. It's like seeing a clay ox or a wooden horse—although you remember the words "ox" and "horse," your mind is oblivious of the reality of an ox or a horse.

9. NINE MEDICINES

Don't take small matters lightly; a small gap can sink a ship. Don't take small things lightly; a little poison can kill you. Don't take small people lightly; small people ruin countries.

---

47. These pairs are terms commonly used in alchemical texts for yin and yang.
48. According to internal alchemical lore, which typically draws on Buddhism, the highest alchemy has no symbol and no process. This is the basis of the doctrine of sudden enlightenment. One of the concentration questions used in Chan Buddhism to foster this perception is "Who is it that is not a companion of myriad things?"

After you can manage small matters, then you can be successful in great matters. After you can build up small things, then you can accomplish great things. After you can treat small people well, then you can associate with great people.

What heaven cannot be sure of is people; what people cannot be sure of is affairs. Leave affairs and detach from people, and the self is in the self. Only what will do will do—there is no imperative to simplify what has to be complex, or to endure what you ought to beware of, or to neglect what you ought to attend to.

Those who are most intelligent know that intelligence is ultimately insufficient to comprehend everything, so they're ignorant. Those who are most eloquent know that eloquence is ultimately insufficient to explain things, so they are silent. Those who are most brave know that bravery is ultimately insufficient to overcome people, so they're diffident.

Of the myriad things of sky and earth, not one thing is our possession. Things are not ours, yet we cannot but respond to them; self is not our self, yet we cannot but take care of it. Though we respond to things, we have never possessed anything; though we take care of ourselves, we have never possessed a self. Don't speak of detaching from self only after detachment from things; don't speak of detaching from mind only after detachment from the body. The Way is one, but you cannot progress in a fixed order.

One who descries the tip of a hair does not see the immensity of sky and earth; one who discerns a tiny sound does not hear the boom of thunder. One who sees the great does not see the small; one who sees the near does not see the far. One who hears the great does not hear the small; one who hears the near does not hear the far. Sages have no specific object of vision, so they can see all; they have no specific object of hearing, so they can hear all.

The eyes see countless objects; some may love gold, some may love jade—this is fixation of vision on one form. The ears hear countless sounds; some may love bells, some may love drums—this is fixation of hearing on one sound. Only sages do not hanker after any object, do not dismiss any object, and do not dwell on any object.

Those who are well adjusted in the present can practice the ancient; those who are skilled at details can establish fundamentals.

Winning by cunning, a thief can catch a thief; enabled by boldness, a tiger can catch a tiger. If you can master yourself, then you can fulfill yourself; if you can transcend things, then you can utilize things; if you can forget about the Way, then you can have the Way.

If a box is hard, some thing will inevitably break it; being rigid, it will crack. When a sword is sharp, things will invariably blunt it; the edge will snap. The awesome phoenix is considered sacred because it is rarely seen; therefore sages make depth their root. Musk deer on the run don't get caught because of the musk they leave behind; therefore sages make a rule of frugality.

A jug has two openings; if you fill it with water, then turn it upside down to pour, if you close up one hole, the water won't come out. That's because there is no descent without rising.[49] On the other hand, even if a well is a thousand fathoms deep, water comes up if you draw from it. That is because there is no ascent without descent. This is why sages do not get ahead of things.[50]

When people make mistakes, though they themselves only suffer the harm after the fact, eventually they consult privately before they make mistakes. Just don't count on your own intelligence, but also include others' intelligence; just unselfishly take the selves of everyone in the world into account—if you practice this all your life, you can thereby avoid mistakes.

The customs of past and present are not the same; the customs of East, West, North, and South are not the same. Even the virtues of each single family and each individual person are not the same. How could we cling to one to predetermine standards for later generations? Just assimilate to customs according to the time, considering potential first and then projects, eliminating anger, stopping greed, simplifying things, sympathizing with people, assessing relative importance before doing things, and you will naturally accord with the inconceivability of spirit and the adaptability of the Way.

There are those who associate through the Way, there are those who associate through virtue, and there are those who associate through affairs. Those who associate through the Way are as father and son, beyond judgment and comparison, hence lasting. Those who associate through virtue have judgment and comparison, so they sometimes join and sometimes separate. Those who associate through affairs are separate even when they join together.

49. The water can't descend out of the jug unless air ascends into the jug.
50. Commentary says this means they "act only when pressed, rise only when moved."

Don't call ineptitude and shallowness the disposition of the Way; it is preferable to be quick and swift. Don't call ignorant dullness the inconspicuousness of the Way; it is preferable to be light and bright. Don't call contemptuousness the loftiness of the Way; it is preferable to harmonize and assimilate. Don't call looseness the broadness of the Way; it is preferable to concentrate intensely. Don't call gloom the silence of the Way; it is preferable to be joyful. The many corruptions in learning of the words of the ancients have to be remedied.

Don't deny society and affirm yourself, don't despise others and honor yourself. Don't use contemptuousness to impute the Way to yourself; don't use slander to impute virtue to yourself; don't use snobbishness to impute talent to yourself.

What stymies the intelligence of all the world is not in intelligence but in ignorance. What exhausts the eloquence of the world is not in eloquence but in being hesitant to talk.

Heaven cannot make the lotus bloom in winter, or the chrysanthemum in spring; therefore sages do not disregard timing. Earth cannot make citrus trees deciduous, or make badgers black; therefore sages do not disregard customs. Rulers cannot make hands walk or feet grip; so sages do not deviate from their strengths. Rulers cannot cause fish to fly or birds to run; therefore sages do not disregard others' strengths. Those who can be thus may act and may refrain, may be concealed and may be revealed; just because they cannot be caught, this is called the Way.

Those of few words are not resented by others; those of few deeds are not criticized by others. People of little intelligence are not belabored by others; people of little ability are not exploited by others.

Practicing it by means of sincerity, carrying it out by means of simplicity, attending to it by means of sympathy, responding to it by means of silence, my Way is inexhaustible.

Make plans with reference to facts, make judgments with reference to principles. Work in concert with other people, achieve in accord with Nature. Facts are informed by the present, principles are informed by the past. Work is in common with others, the Way is up to oneself.

Gold and jade are hard to part with, dirt and rock are easy to abandon. People who study the Way, when they come upon subtle words or wonderful acts, should not get fixated on them. These are to be put into practice, not to be made objects of fixation. If you become fixated on them, no medicine will be able to cure the sickness of your gut and heart.

People who don't understand urgent tasks and instead pursue a multitude of occupations, extraneous affairs, and eccentric interests, will be overtaken by exhaustion and misfortune.

It is a universal pattern that if you abandon familiars for strangers, abandon basics for trivia, abandon savants for fools, or abandon the near for the far, this can only go on so long before it becomes harmful.

Among those who discoursed on the Way in olden times, some spoke of stillness and silence, some spoke of profound depth, some spoke of pure clarity, some spoke of empty indifference, some spoke of obliteration in darkness. Be careful not to shrink back in fear from the ultimate principle of the world when you come across these; ultimately, they are not meant literally. If you know it is not a matter of words or concepts, then you can get what I say in the subtle meanings of those vague expressions.

Sages' great sayings are gold and jade, their lesser sayings are bell-flower and plantain. Used properly, bellflower and plantain will nourish you; used improperly, gold and jade will kill you.[51]

Speaking of a certain matter, party A says it will be profitable, party B says it will be harmful, party C says it may be profitable and may be harmful, and party D says it will be both profitable and harmful. It is necessary to settle on one of these. Those who understand the Way do not speak.

Phenomena have location, and talk of phenomena has patterns. The Way has no location, and talk of the Way has no intrinsic pattern. If you know words have no intrinsic pattern, then all words are the Way; if you don't know words have no intrinsic pattern, then even if you hold to excellent sayings, they become obstructions and cataracts.

It is easier not to believe a fool than not to believe a savant. It is easier not to believe a savant than not to believe a sage. It is easier not to believe one sage than not to believe a thousand sages. One who does not believe a thousand sages does not see others outside, does not see self within, does not see the Way above, does not see phenomena below.

Sages speak of ignorance to get people to be deaf. Sages speak of obliteration to get people to be blind. Sages speak of oblivion to get peo-

---

51. Bellflower can be used medicinally; the new leaves of broad-leaved plantain can be used for food. Gold and jade can kill when they're used for illegal activities such as bribery and espionage, or when greed for them inspires armed robbery or aggressive warfare.

ple to be mute. If one is deaf, one does not hear sounds; if one is blind, one does not see forms; if one is mute, one does not pronounce words. Those who do not hear sounds don't hear of the Way, don't hear of things, don't hear of self; those who do not see forms don't see the Way, don't see things, don't see self; those who do not pronounce words don't speak of the Way, don't speak of things, don't speak of self.

People only know there is true loss in false gain and don't realize there is true loss in true gain. They only know there is true wrong in false right, they don't realize there is true wrong in true right.

Talking about the Way is like talking about dreams: someone talking about a dream says there were such and such gold and jade, such and such utensils and dishes, such and such birds and beasts; the speaker can speak of these things but cannot take them and hand them over, while the listener can hear of them but cannot actually get them. Only good listeners do not get fixated and do not argue. Make your Way round, your virtue straight, your conduct balanced, and your work concentrated.

Printed in the United States
by Baker & Taylor Publisher Services